Praise for

10-8

"A True Cop Book...

I could hardly wait to finish one story so I could get on to the next. Just like patrol—you never know what's going to happen next. "

–Lt. Richard Drehobl
Rosemont (IL) D.P.S.

"Great Stories...

of people's craziness; weird, funny observations on life's little ironies, even profound insights on the human animal. This is the world through cops' eyes."

–Officer Tom Conlin
Las Vegas (NV) Metro P.D.

"Damn Credible Job...

Captures the true flavor of life and death in the field with remarkable eloquence. Cops everywhere will feel a kindred spirit."

–Sgt. Matt Krimsky
San Francisco (CA) P.D.

10-8

A Cop's Honest Look
at Life on the Street

OFFICER X

Calibre Press • Northbrook, Illinois

Published by:
CALIBRE PRESS, INC.
666 Dundee Road, Suite 1607
Northbrook, Illinois 60062-2760
800-323-0037 • (708) 498-5680
FAX: (708) 498-6869

Library of Congress Catalog Card Number:
94-068989

ISBN Number: 0-935878-13-0
Non-fiction

Opinions expressed herein are those of the author solely and do not necessarily reflect opinions of Calibre Press, Inc. Some names have been changed to protect privacy, but the events and individuals described are real.

Printed in Canada

Publishers' Note

This book is bound to be controversial. Some readers—both in and out of the police world—will take strong issue with some of its contents. Some may consider parts of it damaging to the police image.

You'll see that Officer X is far from a saint. He does not always uphold the ideal of police professionalism, nor does he always bow to political correctness. You may not condone his every action or observation, just as we do not.

But today when law enforcement is under more scrutiny than ever before, it is important amidst the din from the media, from the theorists, from special interests, and from policymakers to remember that voices from the *front lines* deserve to be heard.

Officer X is one such voice. He calls it as he sees it, in language of his own choosing, like it or not. What he sees and much of what he feels are shared by thousands like him.

Beneath his flippancy, you can often hear frustration. Beneath his gallows humor, you can hear a struggle to stay balanced in a careening world. And beneath his many warts and scars, you can hear the heartbeat of commitment to an impossible job that few can perform with perfection.

Charles Remsberg
Dennis Anderson
Publishers

To my mother, may she rest in peace, and to all those men and women who have worn and borne the badge with pride and honor.

A Word from the Author, Okay?

10-8 took about two months to write and about twelve years to create. It's kind of surly. It's got kind of an attitude. But, hey, I'm a cop, I'm no Hemingway. I wrote this book in part as a catharsis thing. I thought putting my little stories and opinions down on paper would make me feel better. It didn't. It just made me think more. And when you're a cop, that's not always a good thing.

I also wrote this book because I want people to know what it's like to be a cop. I want people to understand that cops are people, too, with good points and bad points just like everybody else. Some of the things I've written will make people angry, and some things will make people laugh. Some may seem controversial. It's not my wish to create controversy. My wish is that ultimately there will be no crime and that there be peace among men. I hope my words will make cops and non-cops think about our society and how it deals with crime.

I've included tips on crime prevention in this book. This has a twofold purpose. One is to help ordinary people reduce their chances of becoming crime victims. The other is to make our jobs easier. If people would follow some of my friendly advice, I'm sure crime would go down.

Even though I have ten years on the job, I still consider myself a rookie in some ways. On this job something new is always waiting right around the corner. And I hope those words aren't too prophetic. So read on, take to heart what you want, use what you want, and disregard the rest.

I'd like to thank my police department for keeping me gainfully employed for the last ten years. I'd like to thank all of my supervisors for giving me a lot of rope over the years. I'd like to thank the cops I work with and our support group at the department for putting up with all of my little idiosyncrasies. I'd like to thank the people of my town for being basically good people to work for. I'd like to thank God, or whoever runs things, for getting me the job when I really needed it and for watching out for me during the last ten years. And I'd like to thank my father for starting all of this that Friday afternoon in 1982.

The words that unfold before you are mine alone, although in truth I can't really own them. I'm merely responsible for their unique juxtaposition. All of the opinions stated herein are mine alone. They do not necessarily reflect the opinions of my fellow officers, and most certainly they do not necessarily reflect those of my department.

A lot of cops might not agree with some of the things I say. Hey, you guys can write your own books, okay?

Officer X
Somewhere in Illinois

10-8

[Police radio code: "In Service"]

One day after about six years on the job, I was walking by the mirror in the locker room and I noticed something different about my reflection. At first I couldn't put my finger on it. Then I knew. I was a cop. I looked like a cop and I felt like a cop.

10-8

One time I arrested this guy for driving with a suspended driver's license and then promptly backed up into a telephone pole with this poor soul sitting in the back of my squad car. This was in a parking lot, and several people saw me do it. What they didn't see was that I pulled around to the rear of a nearby building and smacked right into another phone pole on purpose to even out the rear bumper. I believe it took me four or five pops to get it right.

10-8

Some things go on in a police department that you just don't want to talk about.

10-8

Many of the guys who install residential burglar alarms have criminal records. Think about it.

10-8

We got called to a domestic disturbance. The woman told us that her husband was out of control. It turned out she had maxed out all the credit cards, and to keep her husband from cutting them all up, she took the cards and locked them in his Porsche. Then she hid the keys.

Her husband calmly smashed the driver's side window of his car with a baseball bat, took the cards out, and cut them up. His cards, his car. Needless to say, no arrests were made.

10-8

Gypsies are bold. They don't hide who they are at all. They dress wild and drive unusual-looking vehicles. But they almost never get caught for committing crimes. That's how good they are.

10-8

It seems like every time a new burglar alarm system is invented, burglars come up with a new way to beat it. Once a guy had a super-duper alarm system installed in his home to protect a valuable coin collection. Burglars defeated the system with a pair of garden shears.

10-8

There are usually three conditions that must be met for a crime to occur. First, there must be a motive or desire to commit the crime. Second, the criminal must have the knowledge needed to commit the crime. Third, there must be the opportunity to commit the crime. If you can put the brakes on any of these conditions, crimes will not occur. Sounds pretty simple, doesn't it?

10-8

Several times I've arrested guys so huge that the handcuffs wouldn't fit. With a guy that big, you pretty much just ask him to come along and we'll try to work it out, okay?

10-8

Once one other cop and I got this extra job guarding Fort Sheridan, an active Army base. Give me a break!

10-8

One time I had a traffic arrest. I brought the guy in, wrote him some tickets, processed him, bonded him out, and typed up the report. Then I went back out on the road. Two hours later I realized I had left my gun back at the station! Our procedure for processing arrestees is to lock up our sidearms in a cabinet so if and when they go ballistic the perps can't grab our guns and shoot us. I guess I just left the station without the damn thing. Thank God nothing happened in those two hours.

10-8

I'm lucky to work in a nice town. There's a town near us where the PD is waist-deep in crime, and they make a lot less money than we do.

10-8

The best crime-busting cops have criminal minds. They just chose to be cops instead of criminals, which is bad news for criminals.

10-8

One of our deputy chiefs was cleaning his gun in his office at the PD. He pointed it at one of his framed diplomas on the wall, pulled the trigger, and said, "BANG!" His pistola also went *bang*, because it was loaded.

10-8

We had a rookie who always put his winter boots on top of his locker. I noticed that he also took them down the same way every time. So I put a cup of water in each boot one time, and he got a little shower. Cops can kid around a lot. You have to. It's a defense against the job.

10-8

One of the bad things about being a cop is that somewhere, sometime, really bad things are gonna happen to people on your beat. Like rapes, assaults, homicides, fatal accidents, child abuse. Our beats are about the size of Brazil. Folks, we can't be everywhere guarding every person or building. I hope you can understand that. A lot of cops can't, and that's where the frustration begins.

10-8

I once went on a domestic that was very unusual, even for our town. A woman called and said her husband had thrown a fake banana at her. I got there and talked with the banana thrower. He told me that he and his wife were involved in a divorce and that he had already spent more than $100,000 in legal fees. They had two very young, very cute toddlers.

10-8

Cops hate defense attorneys. To do their job, defense attorneys have to make their guilty scumbag clients look good and make the cops look bad. The defense attorneys I deal with go easy on me for some reason. Maybe it's because my guests bring them thousands of dollars in business every year.

10-8

I may have generated more than $1,000,000 in attorney's fees so far in my career. So think about it: Who is really benefitting here? Not me, I have to be on the crime scene and again in court, wading through all that shit. The arrestee doesn't get much; he has to pay fines, do jail time, do public service, or pay restitution, plus pay his attorney. All the defense attorney has to do is read the case, look for some loopholes, shuffle some papers around, cause certain people to look bad in court, and put on a good show. He's not the victim of the crime. He doesn't have to be there when it goes down. He doesn't have to go to jail (not usually). He just puts on a suit and takes money.

10-8

We call the hallways in our court building the "Halls of Misery." The only people happy to be there are the attorneys.

10-8

Every police department has those cops who are politically acceptable to the administration, and those who are not. The ones who are acceptable get promoted. The ones who aren't, don't get promoted. I'm in the latter category, for what it's worth. And there are a lot of cops just like me out there. A *lot*.

10-8

I once had a drunk drive all the way onto the grass in his backyard to get away from me. I followed suit, but pulled up closer to the back door.

10-8

Juveniles in our town can commit some pretty good crimes and get away with just a history card in a file and a follow-up interview with our juvenile officer, so it brightens our hearts to see some immediate discipline justly administered by concerned parents in the front lobby of the PD.

10-8

One positive thing about being a cop is that I haven't gotten a traffic ticket in ten years. You figure it out.

10-8

Why does a guy who makes $200,000 a year try to steal a $3.95 pair of pliers from Kmart? It's the thrill, I guess. I just can't see it.

10-8

What's a cop thinking about when he's driving around? Overtime. How he's gonna get some overtime to pay for this or that bill that's coming up.

10-8

We carry rubber gloves, and also keep them at the station, to wear when handling people we suspect may have AIDS or other communicable diseases. Many of our guys, including myself, have been inoculated for hepatitis B. But you still think about getting stuck with hidden needles on car searches and stuff. There are some really bad germs floating around out there.

10-8

Every police department has stories about arrestees who've hanged themselves while locked up in a cell. It happened once with us. These people are under a lot of stress. The ones who are obviously crazy, we ship out to the hospital. But with some people, you just can't tell. We check our prisoners every half hour around the clock, but some people will always find a way to do themselves in.

10-8

I don't know about the full moon thing, but I do believe in streaks. Almost every Sunday is a nice, slow day. But sometimes a Sunday can turn into real hell.

10-8

You'd think that most car accidents happen in bad weather or at night. Wrong. In my experience, most traffic accidents happen on nice, lazy, sunny, summer days when absolutely nobody is paying attention to their driving.

10-8

One time one of our cops wrote this kid up for passing a stopped school bus. A conviction for that offense can get your driver's license suspended. The funny thing is, the kid was sixteen and was on his way home from the driver's testing facility where he'd just gotten his first license. I heard that the license itself was still warm from the laminating machine when our cop took it.

10-8

What lies ahead for the future of law enforcement? "Smart Squads" with on-board computers that can tap into vast data banks for crime statistics, anti-crime technology, local demographic information, criminal history information, motor vehicle and license information, crime analysis and trend prediction, and "Most Wanted" information. How about computers that can read fingerprints in the field, take breath and blood samples, or analyze drug samples? The list of capabilities for mobile computers is endless. Add mobile dish antennas and anti-crime satellites and you're getting a very powerful and effective crime-busting network.

10-8

One morning after a long midnight shift, I was driving by this house in my squad and thought I saw a deer in the backyard. When I backed up to get a better look, I ran over their mailbox! I'd backed up straight, but the street happened to be curved. Good job. The "deer" turned out to be one of those plastic figurines you just stick in the ground.

10-8

For years I've sat out on the highway and pounced on people like I'm some big, fat spider. I think I've probably taken that "these are my streets" attitude a little too far sometimes.

10-8

Have you ever tried to type a detailed report at 3:30 in the morning? I've done it hundreds of times, and I'm tired of doing it.

10-8

Vehicle pursuits are scary. They can end up with the cop getting killed, the offending motorist getting killed, even innocent people getting killed. But, hey, if we just let people drive away, then nobody would stop. So there will always be pursuits.

10-8

One sad thing about being a cop is dealing with homeless people. These people have fallen through the cracks in society because of mental, criminal, or financial problems. Sometimes all three. The most we can do as cops is to get them a free motel room for one night. But what we usually do is just shuffle them along to somewhere else where they'll be shuffled around some more.

10-8

One of the nicest guys I ever met on the job was a guy I arrested for DUI with a revoked driver's license. I brought him in and ran a criminal history check. The guy only had two convictions on his record— both for homicide, and nothing else. Once two guys beat him up at the scene of a car accident, and he shot both of them. In the other homicide conviction, he said a woman tried to brain him with a skillet after they had a fight. When I asked him about it, he politely explained that there was only one thing that made him mad. He was small in stature and was picked on a lot as a kid and abused by his parents. He vowed that when he grew older he wouldn't take it anymore.

10-8

Sometimes I'm accused of picking on certain racial minorities. I will only say that *every* person I arrest has made a conscious decision to break the law at some point and has been caught by me. That is the one thing that all of my arrestees have in common. They're not being arrested because of *who they are;* they are being arrested because of *what they've decided to do.* It's their choice.

10-8

I love it when I stop somebody for drunk driving and I ask them where they think they are and they name a town that's fifty miles away.

10-8

One of my favorite things to do when I'm driving around in the squad and I see people frantically waving at me for something that's clearly not an emergency is to just wave back and keep on driving.

10-8

Cops hate to get involved with other people's problems when they're off-duty. The couple that lives right next to me used to get into a knock-down, screaming domestic about every two weeks or so. I never called my fellow officers. I just listened for a body to hit the floor. Only then would I take action.

10-8

To a cop, there are two reasons why radar detectors exist. One is to allow motorists to break the law. The other is to provide drug money for the young kids who steal them when the idiot who owns a radar detector leaves it out in plain view on the dash or visor. Do I get pissed when I have to take a report on a stolen radar detector? Yes! Do I get pissed when I see a radar detector in a car I've just stopped for speeding? No, because I'm gonna write that guy a speeding ticket.

10-8

I have responded to about 6,000 false burglar alarms and only one real alarm. With the one real one, there was a five-minute lag time in the reporting system. By the time we arrived, the burglars had broken in through a window, snatched a couple of desktop computers, and gone home. Do not expect me to get excited about burglar alarms.

10-8

Never, never say to a cop, "Hey, you can't do that!" Because he generally can, he will, you're done, and it's over, pal. Instead, say, "Can we talk about this?" You have my guarantee that things will go a lot smoother.

10-8

Luck. Lots of times, it's just luck. Once when I was chasing some armed robbers, I had them cornered in traffic at a red light. I do the stupid John Wayne thing and get out of my squad with my pistol out and run up to the back of the bad-guy car. Just as I get up to the rear of the car, a shooter pops up in the back seat. Well, the light changes to green and the bad guys take off, leaving me flat-footed outside my squad. We caught the guys later and it turns out that the shooter had a loaded 9mm semiautomatic pistol on him when I ran up to the car. Just the change of a traffic light probably saved my life. Or his.

10-8

There are many reasons why cops drive fast. We might be responding to an emergency call. The pizza might be getting cold. We might just feel like it. I prefer people think of it this way: Everything cops do all the time is *very* important, and it's important that we get where we're going quickly, thus saving Joe Taxpayer oodles of money.

10-8

If you want to make me mad, send me on a cat call. I love cats, I just don't want to deal with them when I'm busy being a cop. Many times I've had to report that this or that cat escaped my custody and was last seen running west on Such-and-such Street wearing a brown fur coat, et cetera.

10-8

Animal calls are my least favorite calls to go on. We have animal wardens, but lots of times they aren't on duty. So we get stuck with these goofy calls. I will say that they are good opportunities for some positive public relations. Our citizens pay huge taxes, and they deserve something.

10-8

Once, at 4:30 in the morning, I drove up on two guys whose medium-sized tanker truck carrying liquid nitrogen had broken down on the side of the road. The truck was old, and somehow the rear axle assembly had broken off. I called for the big tow truck, but a supervisor came by and the next thing I knew I was working a traffic post, it was 9:00, and 200 hazardous-material personnel were milling around drinking coffee and eating donuts. Finally, one guy walked up to the tanker and drained the liquid nitrogen into the ditch where it boiled harmlessly away. Then the truck got towed.

10-8

We live in an information age. Information is a very powerful tool when used to capture criminals, more powerful sometimes than a gun or a squad or a baton. A cop armed with the right information is unbeatable.

10-8

Once on a traffic stop as I was walking up to the driver's side of a van, I watched helplessly as the van slowly slid backwards and embedded itself into the front grille of my squad. It seems the driver had wakened up his passenger and made him switch seats after I stopped them. The driver forgot to put the van in PARK during the switch, and that's why it slid back. I arrested the guy who ended up in the driver's seat, for DUI. It held up in court because he, for that moment, was in control of a motor vehicle on the highways of this state when he had a blood alcohol content of .10 or more.

10-8

It's very difficult to talk me out of writing a ticket once I've made up my mind. Grave illness will move me sometimes, but there are very few other excuses that will work with me.

10-8

If I ever got caught doing something illegal, I would want the feistiest, nastiest, fightingest, slipperiest defense attorney for my case.

10-8

Why do cops hate change? Because our job is different every day and we like to keep control of as many things as we can.

10-8

Some of our supervisors are okay. Some are absolute jerks. They don't have to be that way to get the job done. That's just the way they choose to be.

10-8

One supervisor drove over the foot of one of our officers. It obviously was an accident, but instead of making out a motor vehicle, injury-accident report (which requires an investigative review), he covered himself by writing it as a public accident (where the paper work is just automatically filed away). I was not impressed. Neither was the cop who had to have his boot cut off at the hospital.

10-8

Discretion. I really like that word. It means that we, as cops, can do whatever we want out there. To a point, of course.

10-8

Nobody in the police academy ever told me that, to some degree, everybody lies to cops. Five-year-old kids, ninety-year-old adults, they *all* lie to us. It took me awhile to figure that out. There's always two sides to every story, and the truth usually lies somewhere in between. When I arrive on a scene, it's up to me to figure out what the truth is, and then make my decisions.

10-8

In a courtroom, the judge is God. I've seen plenty of decisions I didn't like, but I could always see some reason why the judge made that decision. I never challenge a judge's decision.

10-8

Once I was arresting this sailor for DUI. He ran from me and I chased him down an alley behind a grocery store. He was leaving me in the dust when he decided to make a sharp right and run through what he thought were some bushes. What the "bushes" really were was a heavy-duty chain link fence anchored in concrete with bushes growing through it. He broke his nose.

10-8

One time I left my uniform hat in an arrestee's car. He was released on bond and probably drove home. I didn't discover that my hat was missing until the end of my shift. I had his address, so I drove into the city in plainclothes. My arrestee lived in a bad neighborhood behind a grocery store. He had four kids under the age of five. He still had my hat, which he could have tossed or sold. I gave him fifty bucks, took my hat, and got out of there, fast.

10-8

Sometimes people get lucky. A young woman left her car parked in NEUTRAL at a gas station at the top of a hill in the middle of town. It slid backwards out of the station and rolled down our main street for over a quarter of a mile. It ran over the parkway and into another gas station and finally came to rest against an I-beam next to one of the gas pumps. The only casualty was a small dent in her car's rear bumper. No pedestrians struck, no cars struck, no gas station blown up. Lucky. Very lucky.

10-8

Being a cop is different from any other job. When I go to work I strap on body armor, a gun, and a baton. I'm just getting ready for work, but it's more like getting ready for war.

10-8

Tickets. I've written thousands of traffic tickets and lost only four moving violations in court. When I write a ticket, I can sense that I'm putting a small crimp in someone's life for awhile, but I get around it by being very fair. For me, writing a traffic ticket is as easy as breathing.

10-8

Well-being checks are the spookiest. So-and-so hasn't called or been seen or won't answer the phone, so we get sent over. Most of the time the person is well, out of town, at the hospital, the phone is off the hook, or whatever. Sometimes the person is dead.

10-8

One time a hysterical woman called the PD and said that some "strange, white, round things" were in her backyard. The dispatcher had a sense of humor and sent over a lieutenant, who was beyond naive. He came back to the station carrying a plastic bag and wearing a weird, baffled look on his face. He reached into the bag, pulled out this white stuff, and said somberly, "It was moving and just appeared overnight." We could tell that the stuff was just large mushrooms. We laughed a lot about that one.

10-8

Many times the local citizenry, many of whom are city-bred, will call and say, "There's this huge unknown animal in my backyard!" Invariably it's a baby rabbit or a 'possum or something.

10-8

Sometimes when I'm driving around in the squad, kids will give me that focused, I-hate-authority look that I used to give the cops when I was a kid. I understand it, but some cops don't.

10-8

Once I was called to guard the crime scene of an apparent suicide. A depressed young man who was living with his girlfriend put a .22 pistol to his head and pulled the trigger. He died in the hospital. I was there for hours. It's a strange feeling, walking around, poking a little in all the rooms, trying to put the pieces of a dead person's life together. There were many, many letters of encouragement from the young man's family. His girlfriend's parents showed up, and I had to tell them not to take or touch anything. It was sad.

10-8

What's it like to be a cop? Well, there's *us*, and then there's everybody else.

10-8

The worst accident I've handled was a fatality that happened when I had only three months on the job. A guy was going 70 mph in a Porsche down a residential street when he struck another car almost head-on, killing a passenger in the other vehicle. He called his lawyer on his car phone, not the police or an ambulance.

10-8

I once had a guy try to tell a judge that the overhead power lines a few hundred feet away affected my radar. Nice try.

10-8

Every cop has a strategy for staying awake on the midnight shift. Some write parking tickets, some read, some drink coffee or get out of the squad and check doorknobs. I arrest people to stay awake sometimes. But there are times when nothing works. Every morning at about 4:30 there are thousands of good cops on the beat "just resting their eyes."

10-8

Twice I went to work on a midnight shift after partying a lot all day. The first thing I did was to blow on the Breathalyzer machine. I had told myself that if I blew above a certain number I would go home; if I blew below that number I would work. Both times I worked, and both times I arrested two DUIs.

10-8

Cops have many different ways of dealing with the crap they have to wade through. I work out a little, do a little sculpture, and read. When you're a cop, you've got to do something to keep your mind off work.

10-8

When you get suspended, it's like you're not even connected with the department that day or days. No salary, no benefits, no nothing.

10-8

It's been said that cops' kids are the wildest. I don't know about that. But I do know that when a cop gets home after playing Mr. Discipline all day, he damn sure doesn't feel like doing it at home.

10-8

To be a cop, you have to be very tough, mentally. You have to be ready to take a lot of crap without showing any emotion or fighting back. That's hard sometimes. Every once in awhile I get called a pig. I just let it roll off and try to understand where it's coming from.

10-8

There used to be a special place on the edge of an open tract of land where I liked to run radar. It was kind of secluded and I could look straight ahead into a dense stand of four-foot poplars and other trees. I could hear and see the wind blowing through those trees, I could hear and watch the birds. Then the developer virus invaded our town and most of the trees were mowed down to make room for some big, expensive houses. There's just a little stand of trees left. I don't write many tickets there now. I just look at the trees and wonder when they'll be gone, too.

10-8

Often I think about what it would be like if there were suddenly no cops. It would be chaos. Might would make right. We really are a "thin blue line" that keeps the bad guys off the good guys' front steps. Most people prefer not to deal with us, but they need us.

10-8

If you take the cop job too seriously, it can kill you. The bitterness, frustration, divorce, hatred, lawsuits, and ugly cases can all gang up on you and pump a lot of acid into your system. This acid will eat you up.

10-8

We are supposed to be trained professionals. How professional we are or how professional we appear to be can have a great deal to do with how effective we are out there.

10-8

Out of the thousands of traffic tickets I've written, I've written up semi trucks maybe four or five times. Truckers are great drivers. When I do write them up, it's always for the same thing. It's out on the highway, the traffic light changes to red, they're still three blocks away but can't stop because they're going too fast, so they honk their horn a lot, and run the red light. Only then will I give them the banana.

10-8

We had a guy in our town who tried to shoot himself with a rifle, jumped out of a fourth-floor window, slashed his wrists, and ran around in the snow in a bathrobe in sub-zero weather for hours, all on separate occasions. He lived to a ripe old age.

10-8

We had a twenty-one-year-old kid drop dead in the street. An autopsy showed it was possibly some kind of heart problem. The kid had been a problem at one time but had gotten himself straightened out. I guess when your time is up, it's up.

10-8

One time I got this plumbing call. Yes, a plumbing call. It's midnight, it's January, and it's cold. A geezer calls up and says his hot-water heater is spraying water all over the place. So they send me. I hate that. I'm a cop; I carry a gun around, not a pipe wrench. I go over there and go into this guy's utility room, and there's lots of steam and hot water squirting everywhere. So now I'm getting slime and hot water all over me while I'm climbing all over this guy's hot-water heater to look for a shut-off valve. While I'm up there, I happen to look down and see a valve on the wall with a tag on it that says WATER SHUT-OFF in large letters. It's right next to where the geezer is standing, and he's lived there for four years.

10-8

Once I got sent on a call of a white male teen pouring gas on himself at a self-serve gas station. I rolled over there and spotted a guy matching the description walking away from the area. I screeched to a halt, jumped out, and jumped on the guy who, meanwhile, was trying to light himself with a match. My deputy chief saw the whole thing. I saved the guy's life but the DC beefed me for not handcuffing the guy before I took him to the station. (I couldn't because the guy had a cast on his arm from where he'd broken it the week before when he jumped off a bridge.) That guy had some serious problems. So did the DC, now that I think of it.

10-8

Once while searching a tollway spur for a missing person whose abandoned car was found in the area, we found the body of another guy. It was an old man who had walked away from a nursing home in the area and died of exposure.

10-8

The first ten pages or so of the EMT (emergency medical technician) manual deal with liability on the part of the EMT. Sure makes you want to go right out and start pumping on some guy's chest.

10-8

Once our shift commander, a sergeant, got sent on an alligator-in-the-pool call. Please note that I patrol in the Midwest. Our alligator turned out to be a pool blow-up toy about two feet long.

10-8

Don't tempt poor, hard-working, honest people by leaving nice stuff lying around. Your nice stuff will grow legs and walk away.

10-8

Sometimes when I'm on a midnight shift and I find some broken mail-boxes, I try to put them back together to avoid taking reports on kids playing mailbox baseball. Imagine a cop out there with a screwdriver and a hammer in the middle of the night fixing mailboxes.

10-8

At least three times I have gone almost an entire busy shift handling accidents, taking reports, talking to people, et cetera, with my fly open the whole time.

10-8

Sometimes you know there's a loose cannon out there and you can't do anything about it. We had a local guy who went through a bad divorce. Everybody knew he was gonna do something. Sure enough, he showed up at his ex-wife's house and shot her boyfriend with a rifle. The boyfriend lived and married this gal. They now have a family and jobs. The loose cannon went to jail.

10-8

Once I was out on a midnight shift chasing a drunk driver operating a rusty Camaro. It was the first snow of the year, and my squad had bald tires. I failed to negotiate a slight curve at 35 mph and struck a light pole after a skid that seemed to last forever. No damage to me or the light pole. Wish I could say the same for the squad and my ego.

10-8

We have some cops with more than thirty years on the job and many with more than twenty-five. They have my respect for putting up with the bullshit for so long.

10-8

We once had a tornado blow the roof off of a building. A supervisor made a rookie write a report on that.

10-8

I try to learn from the cases I lose. That's the only thing you can do. I also try not to dislike the defense attorneys on those cases, but that's really hard to do.

10-8

I believe in the point system. Everybody starts life with the same number of points. The more crimes that can be tied to you as an individual, the more points are taken away from you and the more restrictions are placed on your personal freedoms. The expiration of all points results in termination or permanent exile.

10-8

One time a local citizen who had a personal problem with me made some wild allegations about me that were totally untrue and then were later recanted by that person. Unfortunately, the local newspaper printed the false statements. My reputation was ruined, and those lies bled over into other areas of my personal life. Is that what I get for the years I've spent laying my life on the line for people every day?

10-8

Once I stopped this guy on the highway for a minor traffic violation. There was something hinky about him; I couldn't put my finger on it. He handed me a valid, recently issued driver's license. As I was checking it out, I noticed that his signature on the bottom was a different name than what was printed up above. The guy had obtained a new driver's license under another name, had a slight mental lapse, and signed his *real* name on the bottom. Under his real name, his license was suspended. So I confiscated his new license and some dope he was carrying, and invited him down to the PD for a chat.

10-8

Once there was this guy who led four of our squads, including myself and one state police car, on a chase up the highway in rush-hour traffic. We got him cornered at a red light, and five of us ran up to the car, which was a new, red Volvo. We were expecting to see an auto thief at the wheel. Instead, it was some yuppie in an expensive suit, in his own car, wearing his seat belt. It turned out he'd lost his job, didn't care about anything, had gotten eleven traffic tickets in the last two weeks, and decided that the next time he got stopped by the police he just wouldn't pull over. I mean, the guy was driving on the shoulder at 70 mph and trying to hit us with his car, too. This was *before* Rodney King, so he got an attitude adjustment while a supervisor just looked up at the sky. The truth is that the fear of video cameras these days keeps a lot of scumbags from getting tuneups they richly deserve.

10-8

One time one of our cops called in sick on a Saturday afternoon. The shift commander didn't believe him and actually went over to this guy's house and walked right in the front door. He caught the cop sitting in his easy chair drinking a beer and watching a game on TV. The shift commander said, "Hey, you don't look sick to me!" The cop said, "Hey, you don't look like a doctor to me!"

10-8

Once I got dispatched to a well-being check where a ninety-year-old woman hadn't answered the phone for two or three days. The door to her apartment was locked, so I did the hero thing and launched myself through an open second-story window. A grim sight awaited: a half-naked, ninety-year-old woman lying on her bed with her mouth and eyes open. The woman was cold and appeared to have been dead for days. I was busy calling the coroner when her mouth moved. I dropped the phone. We didn't need the coroner.

10-8

Once it was so cold on a midnight shift that when I got into my own car in the morning to leave, it took three blocks for the tires to round out from the flat spots, where they'd frozen to the ground.

10-8

There is absolutely no reason why anyone should be allowed to refuse to take a blood test or a breath test when stopped by a police officer. None. You refuse, then we should refuse to give you your driver's license back—forever.

10-8

Our road supervisors have to answer car lock-outs. Some are better at getting into locked cars than others. We had this one sergeant who was just no good at it. Twice he pulled the driver's side window right out of the door. Once he got his lock-out tool so jammed into a car door that he couldn't get it out. Neither could anybody else. So the car owner drove that car with what amounts to a burglary tool sticking out of the door. The thing was in there so long that it rusted. There's a sequel to this. The guy had his car parked on the street in another town two weeks later and a cop saw the tool and called out a burglary-to-auto-in-progress. We straightened him out.

10-8

When you're a cop, violent death can be waiting just around the corner. That suburban housewife you're stopping for speeding could have cracked that day and just shot her husband; you could be next. That suspicious-looking kid with his hands in his pockets could have a gun and a thousand reasons why you, a cop, should not remain standing.

10-8

Things found underneath the back seat of our squad cars: candy, coins, wallets and papers with the arrestee's real name and ID in them, stolen credit cards, switch-blades, marijuana, cocaine, heroin, crack, syringes, LSD, guns. Yeah, think about that last one.

10-8

Once I stopped a car on the highway on a midnight shift. The driver was suspended. The passenger, who was acting a little fidgety, told me that he had to go to the bathroom and started walking towards a ditch. I said, "Uh, hold it a minute." The passenger turned out to be a walking drugstore. A little cocaine here, a little marijuana in this pocket, some pills in that pocket. It went on and on, like Mad Max turning in his weapons in the movie *Mad Max Beyond Thunderdome*.

10-8

There's been a sudden storm and it's over. You're riding your bike down the street, and you see a squad car with its overhead lights on in the road and a cop who's shouting, "Stop, Stop!" at you. Please don't ride over that power line lying down in the middle of the street.

10-8

I've always had a beef with that Fifth Amendment thing about self-incrimination. It just means that people can flat out hide the truth and obstruct justice. I hate that, okay?

10-8

Once I stopped his guy for speeding. He was a well-spoken, thirty-five-year-old white guy, and he didn't have a driver's license. There was something weird about that. So I brought him in and wrote him a ticket for speeding and another for driving without a license. The next month he came to court with a new license. He got a break and supervision. After he paid his fine, he walked right over to me and shook my hand, said thanks, and left. The guy was possibly some safe-cracking ex-con or something.

10-8

We had this guy who was one of the funniest, most obnoxious, rambunctious, rebellious cops I ever met. After sixteen years he made sergeant, deservedly so. But as soon as he got his stripes, he became the meanest, most rule-pulling, getting-good-employees-to-quit jerk supervisor on the face of the earth!

10-8

A favorite thing for truckers to do is to whoosh by a cop on a traffic stop on the highway, going so fast that the cop's hat blows off onto the road where somebody else can run over it. That's okay with me, I hate wearing the stupid thing anyway!

10-8

One night I was chasing a robbery suspect, reputedly armed, across a busy street. I had my gun out, and I may have been shouting the wrong thing as he was running. I think I shouted, "Stop, you mother-fucker, or I'll blow your motherfuckin' head off!" I probably should have said, "Stop, I've got free lottery tickets," or "Stop, my credit is good, and I'll co-sign for a loan!" I was wearing these clumpy boots and fell flat on my face on the ice, in the middle of the street, right in front of some horrified guy driving with his family in their Volvo station wagon. I picked myself up and got back into the race, watched my man hurdle (and I do mean *hurdle*) an eight-foot chain link fence at the rear of a car dealership. We had the dealership surrounded, and a police K-9 yanked the frozen scumbag out from underneath a shiny new Cadillac an hour later.

10-8

I always try to get to the truth in a case before taking any action, but a lot of times that's impossible. So sometimes I make a mistake and arrest the wrong person. I always have the option of making it right at court time.

10-8

If you are a sailor, don't go downtown, get blasted, and then climb all over the outside of the train on the way back to your base. If you do, you're going to be late. And we're going to be busy with you. Maybe *very* busy.

10-8

Every once in awhile I see a red fox or a snapping turtle while I'm out driving around on-duty. It makes me feel like Mother Nature is trying to make a comeback in our town.

10-8

I would never take anything from a house or a business while I was in there alone on an open-door or alarm call. I just can't see blowing my job for a few bucks.

10-8

We have a bulletin board at the PD for the heavy-duty criminals, the ones you see in the wanted posters at the post office. The posters will usually have a picture or two of the guy or gal, and most of the murderers or heavy criminals have a bad look in their eyes. Only rarely will I see a guy or gal up there who looks happy, well-adjusted, or personable.

10-8

The three things that will most likely get you an audience with the local PD: drinking, fighting, and driving, or any combination of the above.

10-8

I have a reputation for being something of a scrounger. One time I piled an entire disassembled slate pool table, with accessories, into and around my personal station wagon in ten minutes, while on-duty and in uniform. I was on my lunch break, of course.

10-8

We have this supervisor, a sergeant, who is a little overweight. Once he tried to kick in the front door of a house on a pretty hot call. It didn't work. He bounced back, and in order to keep his balance he grabbed the nearest thing standing, which happened to be another poor cop. When the sergeant went down, he pulled the cop down to the ground, too. The poor cop hit his head on a tree, and came to work the next day looking like a semi ran over his noggin.

10-8

Every cop who's been around for awhile has stories about when he or she screwed up. One guy was told by a dispatcher with a quirky sense of humor to "swing by such-and-such an intersection and look for a minor accident." The guy got there, and it was a major disaster with cars and bodies busted and lying all over the place. He got so flustered that he got on the radio and asked for a dump truck!

10-8

I don't shout at or lecture my arrestees on the road. I treat them with dignity and use a low-profile. "Okay, we've got a problem, let's go work it out at the station" is my approach. This works very well for me.

10-8

At the police academy, there are many different kinds of instructors.

For the most part, they're good instructors and very into what they're doing. Some were wounded in the line of duty. Some were so wild on the street that the powers that be wisely put them in a safer place. One was a traffic cop who was so slick at taking bribes that they couldn't catch him, so they made him a traffic instructor.

10-8

One time a supervisor and a couple of dispatchers wanted to get this one cop, who was kind of a pain in the butt. Somehow they got the computer to print up that his driver's license was suspended. The supervisor called the dupe in and, with a deadpan face, showed him the computer printout, telling him that because his license was suspended, he couldn't work. The supervisor then asked the guy to turn over his gun. The cop went ballistic.

10-8

I make sculptures out of parts of squad cars that were in wrecks. Many guys aren't real appreciative when I give them one, though. It just reminds them that they screwed up.

10-8

Our job isn't all bad. One guy got fed up with all the crap and joined the paratroopers. One day he found himself sitting in some tent out in the middle of nowhere in a freezing downpour. Two guys in his unit had just died of botulism from eating field rations. Right then he said to himself, "Gee, having court on midnights doesn't seem so bad after all." He came back with us, and he's a sergeant now. Good guy, too.

10-8

There was this cop who worked in the town next to us. He was always "finding" burglaries. He was also having garage sales at his house every weekend, in the same town where he worked. It didn't take too long before somebody recognized some of their stuff at one of his sales.

10-8

If you or one of your whelps dials 911 by mistake, don't refuse to answer the phone if our dispatcher follows protocol and dials you right back. If we do call, let us know what's going on, so we don't have to come to your door and ask.

10-8

Once one of our guys was walking around a house on a residential burglar-alarm call. He absent-mindedly stepped on a pool cover and fell into a swimming pool in the backyard. After he dragged himself out, his partner, who was laughing like a maniac by this time, pointed back to the pool. This guy's gun was lying on the bottom, and he had to go back in the water to get it.

10-8

It's rough being married to a cop. You have to deal with the risks of the job, the lousy hours, the lousy pay, working on holidays, and your mate's constant contact with the public, which includes the opposite sex. It's rough.

10-8

Many times we get gun calls for what turn out to be toy guns. The toy manufacturers have no qualms whatsoever about producing very real-looking Uzis, assault rifles, and semiautomatics. Replicas like that can get a kid killed, just like that.

10-8

One of our guys was working the highway when he saw a car go by with no driver. As he pulled out and got up closer, he saw a dog at the wheel. It turns out that the passenger was a dog trainer and was teaching his dog to drive. Our man wrote the passenger a ticket for allowing an unlicensed driver to operate a motor vehicle!

10-8

Things motorists have used in our town to make a lasting impression on other motorists' cars during traffic altercations include golf clubs, guns, hammers, keys, knives, fists, feet, heads, hatchets, axes, pipes, rocks, bricks, balls, bats, shovels, tire irons, eggs, chains....

10-8

There are people out there who are so nice and pleasant that nobody will ever write them a ticket. These people *do* exist. They're hard to find, but they know who they are.

10-8

I have learned how to do one thing really well since I've become a cop. I can now back up a car with the best of them. So where does that get me? Nowhere, just backwards.

10-8

Things cops do when they horse around: play spotlight tag, drag race, chase each other, hide each other's squads. Stupid stuff like that.

10-8

There is this belief that really good-looking women don't get tickets. I find this to be true, for the most part. A woman who's a stone "10" is hard to find. That kind of beauty is so rare that you want to revere it, to worship it, to idolize it. It's hard to write a ticket to a really beautiful woman because you're looking at the beauty, not the person or what the person did.

10-8

My record for arresting the same person is five. There's about two or three people around town I've arrested that many times. I'm sure they're not happy about it.

10-8

One change I've seen in my career is the number of drunk drivers. It seems like there are fewer of them than in the "good old days." Back then, you could find drunk drivers *everywhere*, flying off the highway, hitting trees, driving in ditches, piled up or pulled off the road, whatever. Now that it's finally become an issue, they've become harder to find. I'm glad when I see more cabs and limos driving around at night. A cab or even a limo costs a hundred bucks, at most. A DUI can cost thousands. I think what's happening out there is good, but it makes my job a little less exciting.

10-8

We had this guy who was exposing himself out on one of our bicycle trails. He must have done it hundreds of times. We got only one complaint from this dowdy-looking gal. She saw him once, then saw him again and called the police. From the description she gave, I nabbed the guy. I can't be sure, but it looked like there were a lot more women on the trail than usual that day.

10-8

Chicago PD, south of my jurisdiction, once picked up this guy on my warrant. They had no charges against him. Their report, written by a rookie, read: "Subject observed by reporting officers lurking in the shadows in an area known to be frequented by drug activity." *Lurking.* I loved it.

10-8

The jail cells at our PD are only designed to hold people for a few hours. There are no lights, no TV, no reading materials, only two metal bunks with pads, a combination sink/toilet thing, and some toilet paper. And we've had people in there for days. I pray to God I never end up in jail.

10-8

It gets pretty lonely when you're driving around town on a cold, snowy night in January and the only tracks you see are the ones you made an hour or two before, when you last drove by.

10-8

I get a kick out of the people in our town who dial 911 and want us to send an ambulance over for their sick pets. They get pretty mad when we tell them to call the vet.

10-8

Although we're apart most of the day, cops are linked quite closely by the radio. Because we have to call to report what we're doing all the time, all the other cops on the shift know everyone else's habits— where they go, where they eat, where they stop. Just one time I called out for my lunch break at a certain park where I'd never stopped before. Every other cop on the shift knew right away I had a woman in the squad. How the hell did they know? You work with guys for years and you get to know each other's habits and quirks real well.

10-8

A lot of TV shows give the false impression that we drive around in two-man squad cars. It just ain't so. Economically speaking, it's usually just *one* lone cop driving around in his little mobile office. It's just him against the rest of the world.

10-8

Once another cop and I were dispatched to a mansion where a doe had tried to jump a low-spiked metal fence and had been impaled. She was still alive when we got there, so the other guy, who really loves animals, had to shoot her. After that we were able to remove her. It was sad to see such a beautiful, wild creature killed unintentionally by the works of man.

10-8

Once I tried to public-assist a drunk. He was acting kind of weird at a convenience store and I just wanted to get him out of our town, so I helped him get his junker started and aimed him in a direction sure to get him out of our city limits in just a few blocks. The plan backfired. He turned around and a little while later floated up on someone's lawn in another part of town. I was mad because I couldn't arrest him for DUI because of what had happened before.

10-8

I'm a cop. I can't be concerned with what leads up to the moment of action in question. I just have to deal with the results, whether that's an accident, a theft, a robbery, an assault, or even a homicide. As cops, we have to wade around in that shit. It's our job. It's not fun, it's not romantic, it's not adventurous; it's *shit*.

10-8

What do you do when you're involved in an accident? Don't wait two weeks and then come into the PD and say, "My insurance company told me to...."

10-8

What do you do if your husband or boyfriend beats on you? Don't just take it. You've got options. One is to call the cops and get the creep charged with assault. You can always decide later to stay together, or you can leave. Just don't let it keep going.

10-8

It's 90° out and humid. Suffocating flare smoke is clinging to my eyeballs, nose, and throat. Traffic is jammed in every direction as far as the eye can see. Some jerk stuck in his Jaguar, fourteen cars behind me, gets out of his car, walks all the way up to where I'm standing, taps me on the shoulder and says, "Officer, I'm in a hurry. Can't you do something?" Sure, buddy, I can make a wish, blink my eyes, and make all this traffic disappear just for you, okay?

10-8

I once stopped two gypsies for a traffic-light violation. They were tenuous suspects in a local driveway resurfacing scam, and I bullied them into letting me process them down at the station. They were not charged and were released by me, as promised. The very next day the two houses closest to the site of that traffic stop were burglarized. Spooky.

10-8

Drug abuse (and that includes alcohol) is far more pervasive than people want to believe. It probably accounts for more than *half* of all crimes. How should we address this problem? I see two options. One is strict enforcement of the law, heavy penalties, fines, et cetera. The other option is regulation. Let the government hand out free drugs to all comers, with mandatory counseling. I know that sounds pretty radical, but the first option doesn't seem to be working.

10-8

The best defense against burglars is to have nothing worth taking. Second best is nosy neighbors. That's the way we catch a lot of burglars. The third best defense may be alarms. Some alarms do help us catch the bad guy, or at least prompt him to go to the next house.

10-8

Every cop fears the stone killer. This is a guy who, as the result of unfortunate circumstances or life experiences or genetics has decided that he (or she) absolutely will not hesitate to blow you or anyone else away. I've only seen one guy like that in my whole career, a guy who took a few shots at one of our cops and was captured a few hours later. This guy had already done time for shooting at a cop. When he got out of jail, he'd gone on a little crime spree. He stole a car in Atlanta, did an armed robbery in Indianapolis, then headed our way. When our guy tried to stop him for a traffic-light violation, the guy had already made up his mind that he was going to shoot first and ask questions later. When I saw him at the PD, he had the look in his eye that said, "I don't give a shit. You get in my way, you're dead." He got ninety years with no parole, because it was the second time that he'd shot at a cop.

10-8

When I see a motorist with a visible radar detector, I like to drive right up behind him and turn my radar unit on and off and on and off, caus- ing his radar detector to buzz, beep, light up or whatever. I will follow the guy and keep doing this until he turns the radar detector off.

10-8

Some houses are plain evil. We had an evil house just east of our southern business district. It was haunted by a child-abusing, drunk father. His wife looked okay, but underneath she was nuts. They had a couple of daughters and a son. The oldest daughter was a chronic runaway and a delinquent with some real problems. Naturally, the house was dark and dirty inside. A teenage kid who was not part of their family died while living in the basement. The kid drank a gallon of windshield solvent. The old man finally died and the house burned down, but the sad memories remain.

10-8

One time I stopped a guy on the highway for blowing a red light. He didn't have his driver's license with him, but the name and date of birth he gave me came back from the Secretary of State with a valid license. I almost let him go, but I was suspicious, so I asked the desk for the physical description on the license. The height, weight, and age were about right, but the valid license said brown eyes. I fondly gazed into the blue eyes of my man and invited him down to the PD for a few tickets, including one for driving while his license was suspended.

10-8

We had this married couple in town. Both were very contentious lawyers, always complaining to us about parking problems and other small stuff. Well, they let a dead tree go for a few years in their backyard. It finally gave up the ghost and fell right onto their neighbor's garage and car. I told the neighbor to get his video camera out and videotape the fallen tree all the way to its base in the lawyers' yard. They later settled in court.

10-8

Let's say you're trying to edge crosswise through stopped traffic near a busy intersection and somebody in one of the stopped cars tries to wave you through. Please don't cross those lanes without looking *first* for cross traffic that the dope who waved you on can't see. You can tell me till you're blue in the face that some guy waved you on, but you're still gonna get a ticket for that little fender-bender you're sure to have.

10-8

I've seen photographs of convicts in prison actually practicing how to disarm a cop. Man, there are some bad dudes out there. Or should I say in there.

10-8

One of our cops shot a suspect last year. This cop was having a little scuffle with a drunk after a chase, and his gun accidentally went off.

He only shot the guy through the shirt collar, though. Close, pretty close.

10-8

Cops end up in the hospital emergency room a lot, usually not for our own problems. We go there to handle attempted suicides, car accident injuries, rapes, assaults, nut cases, fights, other accidents, DUI testing, disorderly subjects in the ER, subjects who were disorderly and then ended up in the emergency room. There are lots of reasons why a cop ends up in the ER, but the one he fears the most is a bullet.

10-8

The Zombie Bandit hit one of our banks in town a few years back. They called him the Zombie Bandit because he spoke very mechanically and always had a blank look on his face. He did about five banks in the Chicago area, four or five in northwest Indiana, and maybe six in southwest Michigan. On a tip from a well-known crime reporting show, Zombie got caught with his wife, holed up in a motel outside of Detroit. He turned out to be a Jewish educator with a bad crack habit.

10-8

One time one of our coppers was down in the basement of this house in town looking for the body of a missing person. Instead he found several large plastic bags filled with marijuana. A judge threw the case out because our man was supposed to be looking for a body, and looking in the bags constituted an improper search. At least the drugs were taken off the street.

10-8

I have plenty of respect for the police officer who stands up for his fellow copper, especially if doing it means taking a long suspension or maybe even losing his job. I've done some things while on duty that I'm not real proud of, things that I want to keep between myself and the other cops who saw me.

10-8

The very first time I got stuck working the dispatcher desk by myself was on a 11-7 shift. At 11:05 this gal called and asked for me. It turns out that when I was investigating a reckless homicide motor vehicle accident during the previous week, part of that investigation led me to a restaurant where this gal worked as a waitress. She really went above and beyond in helping me so I gave her a peck on the cheek right before I left the restaurant. Real professional, right? Well, I was married at the time. I'd been on the desk for a total of five minutes, and this gal was asking me what the kiss meant and all that stuff. All incoming calls to our department are taped, and the tapes are held for thirty days! I was sweating it out on that one.

10-8

Sometimes a guy's hormones will go awry and he'll peep in windows or expose himself. Why can't we ever get a case where a woman is doing that stuff? Don't women have hormones, too?

10-8

One time a drunk came in to our lobby at the PD and tried to order a pizza.

10-8

Every once in awhile, even when I'm trying desperately to keep a low profile, I'll screw up and get called on the carpet. The carpet is that side of the PD where the golden boys and the big brass hang out. I get very nervous when this happens, and for good reason. I gotta go in, bend over, let them take their best shots, and then push on.

10-8

One time our department served a search warrant on a guy we knew was a drug dealer. He was pretty smart. He lived in one side of a duplex, but he kept his dope stash in the other side, out of bounds of our search warrant. He did, however, get pinched for having an unregistered, illegal assault rifle at the time our warrant was served. That held up in court, and he went to jail for it.

10-8

Usually when the offender doesn't show up in court, the case is continued. Sometimes this happens several times, and you've been there each time. But when the cop doesn't show up just once, the whole case can be dropped. Not fair, not fair at all.

10-8

A sure-fire way to end up with more than just one ticket in your hot little hand is to be really verbally abusive to the cop who stopped you.

10-8

In our town a lot of things get stolen out of cars because a lot of people are not too careful about what they leave in their vehicles. My face really turns purple when people start piling on the goods that were supposed to be in the car; like the fur coat, the VCR, the new refrigerator, et cetera.

10-8

These two things really bother me: a guy carrying no ID on him at all, or a guy with too much ID on him. Anybody can make a copy of any birth certificate.

10-8

One time I arrested this guy for possession of a stolen motor vehicle. Right before I was going to process him, I asked him to take off his hat. When he did, I saw a marijuana joint stuck in his hair on the back of his head. I charged him with possession of that, too.

10-8

As a cop, you have to look professional at all times. That means uniforms and lots of rules and regulations concerning grooming. In short, it means that if you are a cop, you have to be well-groomed 200 days out of the year. I hate that.

10-8

This job can be scary. Once I was calmly driving around at the end of a 3-11 shift on a slow Tuesday night. The next minute I'm chasing armed robbers, first by car, then on foot. That's just the way this job is. Everything is cool, then in a split second you're in some very deep shit.

10-8

To be hired onto the job, I had to take a lie-detector test. The lie box guy was real easygoing. I covered up some stuff I did while I was in college, when I was in the I-gotta-swipe-this mode for a short time, and somehow I passed. Later I found out that I wasn't the only cop on the job who did the same thing.

10-8

I've taken hundreds of accident reports. I'm really tired of looking at bent sheet metal and broken plastic. I dream of living in a place where there are no cars at all.

10-8

Once I was first on the scene of a non-fatal stabbing that happened in our housing projects. There was blood on the carpet, blood on the walls, blood all over the place. It looked like the scene of a massacre. A husband and wife had gotten in an argument, then he cut her and left the scene. She was really tough. The offender turned himself in with his lawyer the next day. I could tell that the husband really didn't want to kill his wife, but there was a lot of rage between them. A *lot*.

10-8

A young kid in our town hanged himself just to spite his parents. I guess it worked. He left a strange suicide note, a big paper board that had blessings on it to Prince, Madonna, and such stuff. It made me sad to see it.

10-8

Not all sudden deaths are bad. Sometimes a person drops, and when I go into the house I see pictures and mementos of a happy, family-oriented, success-oriented life. It makes me see that there really are some happy people out there, and even if the deceased is not too terribly old, I don't feel so bad knowing he led a wonderful life and died peacefully in his sleep.

10-8

To be a cop, it helps to be able to say to yourself, "No matter how bad they may be out there, I am gonna be the baddest SOB they've ever seen."

10-8

One of our guys got a sick-bird call. When he got to the area, he pulled into the wrong driveway. He saw a woman across the street frantically waving her arms, so he backed up and pulled into her driveway. As soon as he did, the lady screamed. The sick bird had been lying in the driveway, and our guy had just run over it with his squad.

10-8

One time my authority as a cop was very seriously challenged—by a baby raccoon! I was just trying to shoo it away from somebody's in-ground garbage can, but that little sucker would not yield. I am about six feet tall and weigh about 200 pounds in full uniform. I had a gun, body armor, a baton, and a ten-foot-long, four-by-four wooden beam. I poked that little rascal a few times with the beam, which was a bad move. That monster hissed, spat, and attacked me. After about ten minutes of dueling back and forth, we compromised. It didn't leave, but it did climb up a small pine tree right next to the garbage can. That was good enough for me. I got the hell out of there!

10-8

To trick a burglar, try leaving an empty (and spotlessly clean) mayo jar half full with quarters. The bad guy will pick it up and empty it and leave finger prints on it.

10-8

One time I came on a midnight shift and was told that a cop in a neighboring town had been shot in the leg through a house-trailer door. Stuff like that makes a cop very edgy. A short while later, while I'm on patrol, I see an old pickup truck cross the highway against a red light. The driver pulls into the parking lot of an all-night restaurant. So I cruise up, and as I'm walking toward the driver, who has also exited his vehicle, I tell him about the red light. He raises his arms up, and I see a flash of silver on the left side of his belt. I instantly think it's a nickel-plated, .45 semiautomatic, and my pistol is out like greased lightning, aimed right at this guy's heart. It turns out the guy is a carpenter. The flash of silver was a measuring tape on his belt. Very embarrassing. Did that guy get a ticket? I think not!

10-8

While I was patrolling the highway, this trucker gave up a DUI on the CB. I was in the right place at the right time, and I stopped the offending vehicle. The driver was a very drunk exotic dancer. She was going to be arrested, so I had to handcuff her. As soon as I mentioned handcuffs, she screamed and stuck both arms firmly into the grille of her battered, blue, '78 Buick. Myself and the strongest guy in our department could not pry her off that grille. Finally, we made a deal and told her we wouldn't handcuff her. She told us that six months prior she had been handcuffed and gang-raped by a bunch of drunken sailors.

10-8

Once I had to go back to the same apartment three times in one night on a loud-music complaint. After the first two times, the guy had turned the volume right back up as soon as I was out of sight. The third time, when the guy opened the door, I grabbed his hair and threw him around the room. Not very professional, but it got the message across.

10-8

One of our guys got beefed by a local citizen for eating cherries and spitting out the pits while writing some mope a ticket.

10-8

It's a proven fact that constant shift work takes years off your life. That's what I get for twenty years of changing shifts every month. Just when you get used to one shift, it's time to change over. Sleeping, eating, and recreating schedules all have to change. It's real hard on a body. Come to think of it, so is the pressure, the donuts, and the sitting on your butt in the squad all day.

10-8

Here are some guidelines I use for writing speeding tickets: 0 to 10 miles over the posted speed limit, I won't even pull out. 10 to 14 over, I'll give you a written warning. More than 15 over, and you're gonna get the banana. At exactly 15 over, things can go either way, depending on how I feel that day. Using these simple rules, I can make my mind up before I get out of the car and talk to the motorist. It just makes things easier for me.

10-8

Some guys go out and drink for the entire weekend, every week, and never get caught, for years. One guy goes out one time, on his twenty-first birthday, and gets nailed with a DUI. How do you figure it?

10-8

The two hard-and-fast rules of winter driving are: don't slow down too fast, and don't speed up too fast. Stick with those rules and you'll be okay—unless you meet somebody else on the road who doesn't know the rules.

10-8

I try to avoid arresting women. Women arrestees, especially drunks, are a hassle. They get in your face and whine and yell and whatever. A lot of times, it's just not worth it.

10-8

One time I was working with the fire department on a hazardous-materials spill in the middle of a busy intersection. I had previously spotted a pile of smoking yellow slime on the roadway at that location and we were trying to determine what it was. I was directing traffic and the firemen were busy stringing up a barrier when this gal, who I knew was slightly retarded, strolled right past everybody at the scene and walked right through the spill. We were all waiting for her to drop and everybody was yelling and screaming, but she just kept on walking so we just let her go. The spill turned out to be a little muriatic acid mixed with chlorine. Eventually the firemen just hosed it into the nearest sewer.

10-8

We had this guy on our shift, we called him Crabby. Whenever any citizen asked him for directions he'd say, "You can't get there from here." Then he'd drive away.

10-8

If you're moseying down the road, minding your own business, and you look in your rear-view mirror and see a cop with a scowl on his face, swerving back and forth three inches behind your rear bumper, just get the hell outta the way, even if he doesn't have on his overhead lights or siren. You're blocking progress!

10-8

Helping people break into their own house is a fun thing for me. I've taken doors and windows and frames apart, gotten ladders and climbed in through second-story windows that were open, you name it. I will try for hours to get in. So far I've never been kept out. Cops make the best burglars. Once I was stymied, though, and had a brick in my hand ready to break out a small pane of glass in this door when the homeowner, who was standing right behind me, said something about having the key. I said, "What key?" As it turned out, the person had the key but had tried it and it didn't work. It took me fifteen seconds to get in through the front door, with the key that didn't work.

10-8

Why are some people so surprised when they go away on a long vacation and a pile of newspapers forms magically in their driveway, there's eighteen inches of undisturbed snow in their driveway, and the burglars drive up to their house in a van and cart away everything that's not bolted down?

10-8

One time I was chasing an obviously drunk driver down a residential side street, at high speed. I was yelling over the PA, "Stop, stop!" No good. I even tried, *"Halto, halto!"* I finally got the guy to stop. He was

Polish, fresh off the boat. I guess I'll have to learn to say "Stop" in Polish!

10-8

Once I was taking an injury-accident hit-and-run report in the business district at about 1:30 in the afternoon. My squad was parked in an alley, and as I opened the driver-side door, a Ford pickup truck was right on it. I mean, I opened my door about nine inches and *wham*, I got a truck embedded in my door. Officially, it's my fault for opening my car door in traffic, so I told the pickup driver to beat it. He thought it was his fault, so he was happy about getting a pass. A whole bunch of people saw me let this guy go and they were flabbergasted, shouting, "Hey, that guy just hit your door!" I drove immediately to a secluded park and assessed the situation. The door frame was bent so bad you could see daylight through it and it whistled if you went over 35. So I borrowed a wooden block and a sledge hammer from this guy who had his utility truck parked nearby, and I proceeded to pound on that door. I managed to get it back to where it would only whistle if I went above 55. I got a little lucky on that one. They retired that car from service the next day because it had reached its mileage limit!

10-8

I've thought and thought about our criminal justice system and how it could be improved. The court system is fair, albeit a bit slow. But the penal system, I don't know. Taking a guy, locking him up with only other criminals, and then ejecting that same guy back into society with no job and expecting him not to do a crime again...come on, who are we kidding?

10-8

What is a cop thinking when you see him on patrol on a holiday? He's thinking, "God, I hate working holidays!"

10-8

This lady came into the PD to report that $20,000 worth of jewelry had been taken from her house sometime within the last two weeks. "Where did you keep your jewelry?" we asked. "Under the television."

"Has anybody been near the television in the last two weeks?" "Uh, I had cable installed about a week ago." Oh.

10-8

I once chased a dachshund with three-inch legs for a half mile, in traffic, on a hot Sunday afternoon. I finally cornered it in its own backyard, for God's sake!

10-8

One of my worst days on the job was the day Laurie Dann went on her little rampage, delivering poisoned juice to several places and invading a grade school with a gun. She began early in the morning in our town. I came on at six that morning and was immediately stuck with a serious accident that happened on the midnight shift. If only I had been driving around on patrol I might have stopped her from committing homicide. I cried when I heard that she'd shot one guy and four kids, and that one little boy died. I don't feel half as bad as the detective who'd tried unsuccessfully, for an entire year, to get Laurie Dann's guns confiscated, before this tragedy occurred.

10-8

If you see a suspicious auto, get the license plate. If you're involved in a hit-and-run accident or a robbery, get the license plate. A description like "a blue Chevy" is not real good, okay? Give us a big boost and get the *plate number.*

10-8

I see a lot of repeat customers, guys who are brought in for a variety of offenses in a short period of time. But sometimes something good happens. The guy settles down, gets a job, has a family, and stuff. It's really good to see, but it's rare.

10-8

Most cops will put family before the job. Some don't. They still have the job, but they don't have the family anymore.

10-8

Someone did a study on how long Chicago cops live after they retire. The results were shocking. The average lifespan after retirement is something like sixteen months!

10-8

Will computers ever replace the judge and jury? I don't know. All those variables, along with basic human instinct and a good sense of fair play, might be difficult to program into a computer.

10-8

This is a good story. There was a guy in our area, a very thin, very tall guy who had very small ears. His last name was Bailey and he was in the Army Reserves, so we nicknamed him Beetle Bailey. One day, Beetle got caught in a stolen car in our town. He was only a passenger at the time so he was let go at the scene of the arrest. It turned out that Beetle is a General Motors specialist and can get into any GM product and drive it away in about two minutes. He had actually stolen the car. When we figured this out, we got a warrant on Beetle, who went ahead and stole a car from his neighborhood on Chicago's South Side and used it to drive himself to court on our warrant! Problem was, Beetle got into an accident en route in—you guessed it—our town. So of course he bolted from the accident, stole another car, drove home, and dumped that one by his house. From a description of the hit-and-run driver, we put two and two together, and got another warrant for Beetle. Two weeks later, Beetle gets caught by the Chicago police, after leading them on a chase while he's in a stolen vehicle! They arrest him, but he's such a small-time criminal to them that they release him on a signature bond and turn him over to us. By now, Beetle has been knocked around so much that his left arm is broken, probably from a fall, and he's got a gash in the top of his head the size of the Grand Canyon, probably from the same fall. Some guys just never get the message.

10-8

I hate testifying in a "bad" case where you're sure the guy did it but the evidence is a little weak. You look pretty good after the prosecution examines you and you've got just about everybody on your side. But then the defense attorney digs in. He gets you on a few things. Suddenly, you've lost a few friends. By the time a good defense attorney is done reaming you on a bad case, the whole jury, the judge, and even the prosecuting attorney are looking at you like you're crazy. That's the system. It's certainly more than fair to the offender, but that's the way it should be when somebody's future is on the line.

10-8

One January it was so cold that when I opened my car door in the morning after a midnight shift, the dome light wouldn't even blink on until I was at least three blocks down the road.

10-8

When I first became a cop, I felt funny wearing my uniform, but now that I've been wearing it for twelve years, it feels like a second skin. I can't even tell I have it on.

10-8

Where does the word *cop* come from, anyway? I'm not sure I believe that "constable on patrol" stuff.

10-8

Let me say this as clearly as I can: You run from the police, and you're gonna eat lunch! You risk your own life, the cops' lives, and innocent people's lives when you don't pull over and take your arrest like a civilized adult. People can whine all they want, but I'll say it again: You lead the cops on a chase for more than a few minutes, you deserve what you get.

10-8

Some days I go to work and I feel like really getting after it out there. Other times, I just want to get in my squad, go somewhere private, and go to sleep.

10-8

Sometimes on a midnight shift I turn on the CB in the squad and listen to the truckers. Why do they all sound like they're from Alabama? In the middle of the night they talk about cops (they call us bears), weigh stations, work, trucks, loads, women, what the President is doing, the economy...you name it, they talk about it. Sometimes they tip me off to a DUI headed my way.

10-8

A cop's primary directive is to protect lives and save property. I will say that when I'm out there, I don't think about the primary directive all that much.

10-8

Okay, let's say I'm out on patrol. You're approaching a stoplight that's in the process of changing from green to red. You've made up your mind that you are going to run this light. At the last second, you see me sitting there and stomp on the brakes, thus skidding right through the intersection. My favorite reaction is to get out of my squad and applaud after you come to a stop. Rarely will I give you a ticket because, hey, you tried!

10-8

One time I picked a stuffed monkey out of somebody's garbage, and left it handcuffed in the rear of a supervisor's squad.

10-8

My dad started it all by handing me the want ads on a Friday afternoon back in January, 1982. He said, "Here, try this." Little did I know what I was getting into.

10-8

As a cop, I have to respond to bad accidents of any kind. Once I was dispatched to a bad industrial accident at the plastics factory across the street from our PD. A worker was up at the top of an extrusion machine, where he'd been trying to clear an obstruction in the bottom of the hopper while the machine was operating. He got his hand caught in the impeller screw and it pulled his entire forearm into the impeller chamber. It took mechanics and paramedics over half an hour to dismantle the machine enough to get this guy's arm out. He was in great pain. His hand and arm were mangled severely. It was not a pretty sight. I won't ever forget it. I used to work in a factory.

10-8

Here's another pain-in-the-ass accident. For some reason, an old guy stomped on the accelerator in his station wagon while sitting outside the service bay at our local Lincoln dealership. He flew around the building and played pinball with six brand new Lincoln Town Cars on the north side of the sales lot. There was so much damage that my hand got tired from writing the report. When the dealership called about a week later, wanting me to add another car to the report, I said, "No way!"

10-8

There was this guy I arrested once for driving with a suspended license. He drove by me again about eight months later. He looked familiar, but I couldn't place him, so I waited for probable cause and put a traffic stop on him. He was still suspended, and pretty mad, too. He told me he had a lot of construction work in the homes around the police station. To keep me from recognizing him, he'd repainted his pickup truck another color, shaved his beard, and gotten a haircut, because he "had" to drive. I still nailed him!

10-8

I've found some strange things on the road, but the strangest was a battery-powered portable vagina, batteries included. We have one supervisor who's a potty mouth and he was our shift commander that night. I brought the thing into the station and put it on his desk when he was out on a call. He says he threw it out, but I don't know.

10-8

I don't have much respect for guys or gals who spend hours and hours every day drinking in some bar. What kind of life is that?

10-8

Guns. When the Constitution was written, the early settlers faced danger on a frequent basis from hostile American Indians, invading armies, animals, and desperadoes. Not to mention the need to hunt for food. The right to keep and bear arms was essential to their survival. Today, we're almost all crammed into this urban setting. We don't need to hunt for food. We killed most of the American Indians and isolated the few who were left. The odds of a pending invasion are mighty slim. And the wolves, bears, and pumas aren't around, either. So we really don't need guns, do we? Unfortunately, there are a lot of other dangerous "animals" around that we have to deal with.

10-8

One time this scammer gal called one of our fur stores in town and ordered a mink coat, billing it to the credit card of one of our locals. The fur store delivered it to the caller without ever seeing her. They sent it to some bogus address on Chicago's South Side. Fur stores, don't do that!

10-8

Most kids go through a stage when they do some minor crime for a-while. For about a year we had a car-hood-ornament theft ring operating in our area. The kids got caught, and through some excellent investigative work, the "ring" was decimated.

10-8

There are guys out there who make a living stealing tires and radios from new cars. What a way to live, what a great job. I can just see it. Dad wakes up, has dinner, kisses wife and kids, grabs his burglary tools, heads for the door and says, "Bye, honey, I'm probably gonna be late for breakfast. I've got the Schmuck Motors job tonight, and it's kinda far away...."

10-8

A scary moment for a cop is getting called in off the road to see the deputy chief when you know you've violated about a thousand regulations in just the past three days!

10-8

Another low point in my career was when George Bush was vice president and decided to come to our town. Right when his motorcade reached my traffic post, this old lady, against my hand and whistle and whatever, pulled right past me, directly in front of the whole shebang. Luckily, she was far enough in from the Veep's limo so that an Illinois state squad car was able to hustle her buns the hell outta the way.

10-8

We once had one of our coppers solve a major—and I mean *major*—case, just by watching TV. He was watching the news when he saw a vehicle that was involved in an attempted abduction in Chicago. The description of the vehicle and the offender matched the description we had for an abduction-rape-attempted murder that had happened in our town but started in Chicago. Our victim positively identified the guy. Television is a powerful medium for that stuff.

10-8

The judges in our court system are very fair and smart. I have a beef with only one. He was a state trooper before he became a temporary judge. I lost a couple of DUI cases when he believed the offender instead of me. And twice, once on a stand-up speeder and once on a stand-up stop-sign ticket, he let the violator off because "it was my turn." My turn for what? I see him in court all the time, and he gets mad when I don't talk to him.

10-8

Total number of ideas suggested by our supervisors and implemented by the administration to the benefit of our department in the last ten years: Zero!

10-8

I've been eating those deli sandwiches every work day now for about three years, ever since my divorce. Hey, there's only three or four different kinds. You got your roast beef, turkey, ham and cheese, and tuna salad. Jesus, I'm tired of deli sandwiches.

10-8

Some of my favorite cases are when kids do a theft or a vandalism and then walk straight home...in the new-fallen snow.

10-8

I've made thousands of traffic stops, but besides armed robbers and obvious stolen autos, I've rarely had anybody try to get away from me. Of course, I wait until I'm right on top of somebody before I turn on the overheads or siren. Once it looked like a guy was trying to get away from me, sneaky-like, but he got stuck in heavy traffic on the highway.

10-8

If you're some young stud and I stop you for speeding, don't tell me your girlfriend's having her period and needs to get home *right away*. I don't care about your girlfriend's period, okay? And I don't think you do, either. Here's your ticket.

10-8

One time I arrested this guy for driving with a revoked license. My original probable cause for stopping him was to issue a speeding ticket for going 3 mph over the posted limit. I tracked him on a pace no less, not on a radar. I'm not real proud of that.

10-8

If you have an animal or a bird in your house and you don't want it there, why don't you just open the door or a window or two and let the damn thing out, okay?

10-8

It takes awhile for motorists around here to get into the mode of winter driving. Either the first four inches of snow of the year or that last nudge at the end of April catches our drivers completely out of sync. When that happens, cops beware, because it's a demolition derby out there.

10-8

One time I went on this ambulance call where an eighty-one-year-old guy fell down the stairs. We all get there and the paramedics run an EKG strip on the guy. We're all looking at the scope and instead of regular pulse beats we're seeing something that looks like Chinese. But the guy is fine, he's not hurt, he's sitting up and talking to us. But he should be, like, dead. They had him sign a release, and we all left.

10-8

I once got sent on this raccoon-in-the-bedroom call at 4:30 in the morning after a long midnight shift. I get there and it's an old geezer with his even older geezer father living in this old house with a hole in the roof. A baby raccoon had fallen through the hole into an upstairs bedroom, and the two of them had been torturing it, poking it with a cane and shooting it with a pellet gun, for hours. The poor thing was squashed behind a radiator and would not budge. I grabbed it by what I thought was the scruff of the neck but what turned out to be the scruff of the behind. The raccoon turned and bit me on the finger. Naturally, I let go of it. I looked around the room and saw there was a door to the outside. As soon as I opened it up the raccoon smelled the outdoors and left. However, the rabies shots were painful and cost the city about $1,500. I love animal calls.

10-8

Once I went on this burglar alarm call at a posh house that had a security gate. When I got there, the keyholder told me to park my squad in the gateway so the gates would stay open. After we checked the house and I got in my squad to leave, she closed the gates right on my squad! I tried to back out real fast, but I didn't get out in time. The right gate hooked onto my front bumper and yanked it out about three inches. I took the squad into a park, put a blanket over a concrete wall, and rammed my vehicle into the wall until the bumper was back in place. When I was finished, you couldn't even tell anything had happened. Once again, successful body work.

10-8

Gypsies are a fascinating people. Some are professional scammers from a closed society, and they're taught from day one that there are two rules in this world: One is that the world is made up of quick people and slow people; two is that the quick people sure as hell better take advantage of the slow people. Some gypsies are so slick that sometimes it takes days before people know they've been had.

10-8

What do you do when you come home and your house has been burglarized? Don't even go into the house, because the burglar could still be in there. Don't clean everything up and call the cops the next day. If you do, you'll probably ruin any evidence that we could use. Go to a neighbor's house and call us right away.

10-8

Let's say you messed up on the road, goofed, weren't paying attention, and then you see a cop's red lights come on. The cop walks up to your car and, before you can even get your whole excuse out, you notice that the cop has turned purple, thrown his hat on the ground, and is shouting stuff like, "Who do you think you are?" Remember that almost all cops are people, too. We have our good days (rare), our bad days (most of the time), and our bad-like-hell days (once in a while). People expect professionalism *all* the time. But just try to understand anyway, okay?

10-8

Drugs are a real problem today. I'm one cop, one person. I don't have all the answers, I just have a job to do, to keep an eye on my streets and on the people in my town. But I wish to God somebody would do something instead of just giving lip service to the drug problem.

10-8

Every once in a while I have to arrest a junkie. Junkies can be black or white, male or female. They usually have very long rap sheets. Sometimes they have AIDS and fresh sores and infected forearms from bad needles. You have to get real close to process them. When I'm fingerprinting them I'm thinking, "Once this was a person with a family and hopes and dreams. Now I've got a zombie on my hands who will do anything, maybe even kill somebody so he can get high."

10-8

It's frustrating when you know who committed a murder, and why, but you don't have enough evidence to prove it. You only hope that justice will be meted out some other way.

10-8

I know it's not right, but I still have real trouble with that "innocent until proven guilty" stuff. We investigate, arrest, and jail people who we believe are guilty before they are ever tried, so what does this mean? Getting off is so easy, it almost makes a cop want to go out and commit crimes just to prove the system stinks. Are we being too fair with the criminal element in our country?

10-8

I was once dispatched to a man-down-in-a-stairwell call. When I got there I saw a homeless man, who we knew, lying dead on the stairs in the vestibule of an apartment building. There was no one to care, no one to grieve the passing of this human being. We called the coroner, and he came and took the body away.

10-8

I once arrested the same guy twice in one night for DUI. I'm not real proud of that. When I first arrested the guy, I made the mistake of letting him go on a signature bond with the understanding that he would not drive. I told him to his face, "Don't drive!" But he went back to his car and drove, so I arrested him again for DUI and charged him all over again.

10-8

The only time I get beefed by citizens is when I give them a break. Why this happens, I can't tell you.

10-8

Suicides are hard. A lot of times, the people had at least *something* going for them. It just makes you think that if only one person had been in the right place at the right time, an unnecessary death could have been prevented.

10-8

As a cop, I see, and often have to deal with, people I know for a fact had great potential at one time in their lives. But they let drugs or alcohol take it all away. Drugs seem to burn out a person faster, but alcohol can do the same thing.

10-8

So you're involved in a motor vehicle accident and the other party is getting antsy and wants to leave. Unless he or she is a close relative, just say, "I have your license plate, vehicle description, and I know what you look like. You leave now and I'm calling the cops, and they'll be on you so fast your head will spin, okay?"

10-8

I once chased a fifteen-year-old kid two blocks, for shooting off fireworks in a schoolyard. When I caught my guy I stayed pretty cool. I only shoved his head in the mud *once.*

10-8

Once on a midnight shift I was driving by this short dead-end street when I thought I saw red taillights in there. I stopped, turned around, and pulled in. There was this new pickup truck, half in and half out of a driveway in the cul-de-sac. This guy, who is obviously drunk, waddles over to me, says he has a flat tire, and asks me to give him an escort home. I say sure, so then he gets back in his truck and starts driving. He has a flat front tire, so he's driving all over the road. I waited a few blocks and then arrested him for DUI and driving with an unsafe tire! He was only twenty-two years old and already suspended for a DUI.

10-8

We have this town nearby where things are really rough. They're so bad that they have a special initiation for rookie coppers. Take a rookie named Steve, for instance. On his first day, Steve's field training officer says, "Look, when we're on a traffic stop and I call you by anything other than your first name, kill the driver, okay Bill? That is your first name, isn't it? I have trouble remembering names you know."

10-8

I can tell when I'm dealing with people who were abused as children. They have only one reaction to frustration: Violence.

10-8

I've dealt with a few kids who were just evil. They are most frightening to me. They come from extremely wealthy families and from very hard-working middle-class families, too. Exactly where their hatred and their keen desire to hurt others and break the law comes from, I really can't say. I'm just a cop who has to deal with their evil ways. You can't lecture these young people because they are already too far gone to care.

10-8

We were once shown a picture of the ultimate drug addict. The subject appeared to be a young white woman. Her entire body from head to foot was covered with large, ulcerated sores. There was a sore on her hip an inch and a half deep and the size of a salad plate. A narcotics detective said that in her final days she would just lie on one side and pour heroin directly into that large sore to get high. I'll never forget that.

10-8

When cops go to court, it seems like we're always the ones who get reamed. It's always what *we* did that gets the most attention, not what the bad guy did. It took me awhile to figure it out, but that's the way it should be. When we arrest and charge someone with a crime, we are ultimately affecting that person's personal freedom. I hate like hell to admit it, but what cops do should be questioned, a lot.

10-8

Once I got a call at 4:30 in the morning about a suspicious auto in somebody's driveway. I thought it would be a limo or a cab or the newspaper delivery guy. The complainant's driveway was 200 feet long. I drove all the way to the end near the house, and there's this rented Lincoln running but backed over some bushes. I know right away that I've got a drunk. But he's on private property, and you can't arrest someone for DUI if he's sleeping in a car in someone's driveway. So I pounded on the driver's window and said, "Get outta here!" Then I ran back to my squad and waited for the drunk to pull out onto the road. I bagged him a few blocks later, after the guy drove over the center line one time. He never knew what hit him.

10-8

Not once but twice in one night, I went to the wrong house on a burglar alarm call. Both times the front door was open and I walked in the house, went upstairs, and saw people asleep in their beds before I figured out I was in the wrong house. That was a weird feeling. I just backed up and got out of both houses without waking anybody up.

10-8

I enjoy it when guys try to lie to me about their names. The guy's an obvious scumbag, yet no criminal history or driver's license information comes up on the computer? Come on! I figure the guy's lying and take him to the PD. Then I dig around a little or maybe fax his fingerprints to the FBI and find out who he really is.

10-8

Our policy is to fingerprint all arrestees. We take a set of fingerprints and a palm print. Once, as a joke, I told this guy with a scar on his chest that we had to get an impression of it for our files. So I took the ink roller and rolled his chest, then took a palm print card and stuck it on there. It worked pretty good!

10-8

What do I do when a motorist I'm giving a ticket to explodes? I stand back and let him or her vent till they're through. Nobody likes getting a ticket. I know that.

10-8

I love it when the driver of a car I'm stopping for a traffic offense changes seats with the front passenger as I'm walking up to the car. I don't waste any time. I just walk around to the passenger side and ask the person who was driving why he or she doesn't have a driver's license. I had one gal slide from the driver's seat into the back seat in about a second and a half. She must have practiced that one!

10-8

They say a good cop never gets cold, never goes hungry and never gets thirsty. I try my best to live up to that.

10-8

One of the worst things about being a cop: having to get up and leave right in the middle of a great party or a warm family function, and go to a job where I make people miserable. Great, just great.

10-8

One thing I've got to do at work is calm down my driving in general and quit driving like a maniac and taking a lot of chances just to make some goofy traffic arrest.

10-8

It's been rumored that the radar signals from our radar guns can cause cancer or sterility. I hope not. My kids, at least, turned out okay. But you won't see me holding that radar gun between my knees anymore, that's for sure.

10-8

If you're a cop, you'll never be rich. But you won't be poor, either.

10-8

I love 25 mph speed zones. We even have one 25 zone that's downhill! Nobody in his right mind can drive 25. Some cars won't even go that speed without stalling or without the driver having to ride the brakes.

10-8

Quota? There's no such thing as a quota! We do not have a quota. We have a "suggested minimum." New guys go out and try to change the world, so they write twenty or thirty tickets a month. Older guys with a lot of years on just want to retire, so maybe they write two or three. Our suggested minimum is eight moving violations a month, which averages out to about one every two and a half working days. Quota. Hey, come on.

10-8

Women cops who can do the whole job? I've seen 'em, but they're rare, really rare. More rare than you might think.

10-8

You've just made a very stylish U-turn in front of a No U-TURN sign posted in the town where you've lived for many years. If I stop you, please don't say, "Officer, why are you stopping me? Did I do something wrong?" Yes, you've done two things wrong: the U-turn you just made, and what you just said to me. And by the way, where is your current city sticker?

10-8

Part of a cop's job is sudden-death notifications. That's when two cops are standing at your front door, and you get that ominous feeling, and they start out by saying, "Ma'am, I regret to inform you that...." Do you know why there are always two cops? Sometimes the receiver of the bad news goes ballistic on the messenger. We get some strange reactions. I don't blame those who don't react in front of some strange cop. Sometimes it takes awhile for the full impact to sink in.

10-8

Once, for some unknown reason, my star was rising and the department decided to send me to the National Crime Prevention Institute in Kentucky. I had a ball for three weeks and learned a lot. Before I went, the administration promised me I would be the department's crime prevention officer when I got back. Crime prevention was a coveted inside job with regular 9-to-5 hours and weekends off. Mysteriously, my appointment was postponed several times and finally they took another cop who already had an inside job, and made him crime prevention officer. Go figure.

10-8

Although I have many serious beefs with our supervision and administration, I am still proud of the job our department does on a day-to-day basis.

10-8

I'm in excellent physical condition. I have a bachelor's degree in general management from Purdue. I'm a sensitive guy who can make a decision out there, who can be fair. I'm not afraid to get in a scuffle. I have loads of specialized training. In short, I'm everything you would want your local cop to be. Uh, did I forget the part about being crazy?

10-8

I figure that I've generated about $500,000 in fines from tickets I've written and arrests I've made. I've cost the city about that much in salary and benefits. So I've been working for free, right?

10-8

There was this serial killer who maybe did one of the kids from our town. Some good cops catch the guy with a bloody knife and some rope in his truck, but a judge cuts the guy loose because of an "improper search." So the bad guy promptly goes out and slices and dices a sixteen-year-old kid. Following the precise letter of the law with a guy like that is a real dilemma.

10-8

Something that really makes me mad: I'll be driving like a maniac trying to catch some violator and some other person will yell at me, "Slow down!" You try to tell the cops what to do without having any understanding and you're gonna get all kinds of attention you don't want.

10-8

Many, many times I've come across people who have been arrested more than 100 times. Jesus, what's a person like that doing out on the street? Career criminals should be sent to an island for the rest of their lives. Drop them in, drop them a little food and some essentials, but mainly, just let them live their lives among their wretched selves and keep them away from decent people.

10-8

I once helped a guy who had run out of gas. I helped him because I knew he was drunk. I even made one of my plastic street guides into a funnel so that this guy could gas up. I got gas all over my hands. When he drove away, I followed him for about four blocks before arresting him for DUI.

10-8

I once arrested this gal for driving with a suspended driver's license. While I was processing her, she made me an offer. I took her up on it.

10-8

Another great moment in policing: I once got assigned to guard the buses of the Israel Philharmonic Orchestra against possible Arab missile attacks.

10-8

Let's say you've just had an accident. You know for sure that you did not cause the accident, but the cop has your driver's license and it looks like you're going to get the ticket. Please, before the pen hits the paper, attempt politely to re-explain what happened in the accident, or ask the cop to get out of the squad and take a look at something. We are obligated, and rightly so, I believe, to write a ticket at every accident. I really would prefer to write the right ticket for the right offense. But sometimes I make an improper assumption. Sometimes I will not listen to, or get the whole story from, one participant in the accident. Even a minor detail, if overlooked, can cause me to make an error. Details, such as the speed of both vehicles before the accident, the exact point of impact, whether they were moved after the accident, traffic signals and signs, can make a difference in the report and help determine who gets the ticket.

10-8

One time this five-foot, 100-pound gal from Kentucky stared me right in the face and said, "I wanna kick your ass right now!" This admiration was sparked by a DUI arrest of that person, by myself. I'm glad my supervisor was there, or she might have done it. Or tried to.

10-8

I once closed my squad door on my finger after getting out at a traffic stop. I still can't figure out how I did that.

10-8

True story. We had this cop giving a local citizen a speeding ticket. The party was giving the copper a hard time, which prompted the cop to say something about shit happening. At precisely which time bird-shit landed on the cop's right shoulder!

10-8

Over the years I have honed to a T one remarkable skill. I can now hold a quarter-pounder with cheese in my right hand, a vanilla shake in my left, and a large fries in my lap, and consume them all while maintaining vigilant motorized vehicular patrol.

10-8

One time this local scumbag decided he was going to resist arrest at our station. It was shift change, so we had twice the usual number of officers within about ten feet of the guy. Bad move, very bad move.

10-8

Once I got sent on this dog-bite call down in our business district. The victim was already at the hospital when I arrived on the scene. The guy who was babysitting the offender, a large male Rhodesian Ridgeback, had the critter on a leash and was slowly letting it come up to sniff me. Well, the sucker lunged suddenly and chomped me on the abdomen before its tender could pull it back. I was so ticked that I called for a backup right away, to keep myself from shooting that damned dog. Luckily, it had caught me by the lower edge of my body armor so the only damage I suffered was to my ego and to my uniform shirt, which was torn to hell.

10-8

I believe firmly in the death penalty. You do somebody without a good reason like self-defense or years of abuse, you should be done yourself. That's simple enough. I don't care if it's a deterrent or not. I don't care about poor impulse control. I don't care about crimes of passion. I don't care about murders committed because of alcohol or drug abuse. You kill some member of the human race, you should be ejected from the human race, *immediately.*

10-8

The driver of every car I've stopped with New Mexico plates has been driving with a suspended driver's license. That's really strange. I lived in New Mexico once, too.

10-8

Don't ever bounce off a curb while driving in front of me after dark. If you do, I'll arrest you for DUI, and you will blow a .18 on the Breathalyzer. Yet another quirky thing.

10-8

It's so easy to steal a car nowadays. In fact, it's so simple that there are people out there who aren't real smart who steal a car, take it to where they want to go, dump it, steal another car nearby, take it to where they want to go, dump it....

10-8

Cops used to be able to call the phone company to get information on unlisted phone numbers for emergencies or investigations. All we had to do was give our department phone number and personal ID, and the phone company would call back confirming who we were and give us the information. Now we can't get the information at all. We have to go through our supervisor, then through their supervisor, and we still don't get the info unless we get an act of Congress. This is very frustrating. It's as if cops only use their very limited authority to get non-public information for personal reasons. We would never do that, would we?

10-8

One night when I was at the station with a DUI arrest, opportunistic tire thieves made off with about forty-four tires from a used car lot in my beat. The lot was right on the highway and one mini pickup truck parked five feet from the roadway was up on milk crates with all four tires missing. It was pretty embarrassing. But I will say one thing: I will give up one, ten or even 1,000 tires just to prevent one injury or fatal accident caused by a drunk driver!

10-8

The Rodney King beating was bad for all cops. A lot of coppers feel that if you lead them on a chase and you're drunk or on drugs or both, you deserve to eat lunch when you're caught. But what I saw on the tape went beyond that. When a cop is involved in a motor vehicle pursuit, the adrenaline takes over. We are not in control of our brains; chemicals are. Add that to the race thing and Rodney's behavior, and you've got the potential for something bad to happen. But in Los Angeles the additional factor was mob psychology. On the videotape, it looked like there was nothing but cops on the scene. So on top of everything else, you get the "we're righteous, we're pissed, this is a crazy black man here, it's only us, so we're gonna do what we have to do!" Pay particular attention to the *we* word. Also notice how I use the word *we* a lot.

10-8

One of our local citizens put his briefcase containing $20,000 in cash and checks on top of his car, then drove the car off to work. The briefcase and contents were never recovered. Our only clue was a local who reported two guys in a public works truck picking up something from the roadway in that area, at about the right time. We happen to have a lot of guys working for public works.

10-8

One change I've seen over the years is the tremendous increase in check and credit-card fraud. That's because it's so damn easy. Please, banks and shopkeepers, check photo IDs and save yourselves, your clients, and the cops a lot of trouble and money.

10-8

There are some supervisors on my department who think I would arrest somebody just to get out of special duty or paperwork. Not true, not true!

10-8

Dusting for fingerprints is a real pain in the ass when you don't know what you're doing. The fingerprint powder is very fine and very black. It gets in your eyes, your nose, and all over your wrists, hands, arms, and everything else, sometimes even what you are supposed to be dusting. And it doesn't wash off. Lots of times I've walked around all day with fingerprint powder all over my face.

10-8

Say one day you look in the mirror and notice that you're wearing a helmet made of tinfoil to block alien transmissions from being beamed into your mind. Let's just get a little help, a little counseling, okay? Don't go out and cut your neighbors' TV cables in an effort to reduce incoming alien transmissions. Because your neighbors are going to call us, and we are going to have to come over and take you and your tinfoil helmet away.

10-8

A lot of cops only have friends who are cops. It's like only we can understand the kind of stuff we have to put up with. And the shift work kind of puts a crimp in joining the baseball team or bowling league or anything that meets at a regular time for more than a month.

10-8

There are a lot of law-abiding, cop-loving citizens out there, people who really appreciate what we do and help out when they can. God bless them. May they be fruitful and multiply.

10-8

I think of man as being like a virus. He ultimately destroys his local environment and then moves on to destroy another local environment. The only difference is that a man can choose to be a beneficent virus. He has the ability to arrive and *improve* his environment.

10-8

In Chicago, the cop job is considered to be a good job. In our town, we're like everybody's servant or doormat. We make a lot more money than Chicago does. Some days I wish I had the respect instead of the money. Except on payday, that is.

10-8

We had a child-abuse case where a two-and-a-half-year-old kid died. His parents brought him into the emergency room with the story that he fell down the stairs twice while riding in his little car. Turns out that the kid had just come from California and was having a little trouble adjusting to the move. It took the father two weeks to beat the kid to death. I think the father got life and the mother got twenty-five years. This stuff is happening everywhere, right under our noses.

10-8

The Officer X Principle: The more people you get living in one area, the more complicated your interactions get, the more rules you gotta have to govern those interactions. Which means that to be truly free, we're gonna have to spread out and simplify, or go mad. Think about it.

10-8

A defense attorney has been concentrating on your case for days. He wasn't there when things went down, so he has to make up stuff and believe whatever his clients tell him. And he has to confuse you on the witness stand. And you, the cop, are usually working midnights and you haven't really studied the case and you're supposed to remember every little detail about some arrest that happened over a year ago?

10-8

Several times a year I get stuck being awake for more than twenty-four hours straight. I hate that feeling. It's like being dead. It just works out that way, and there's nothing I can really do about it. I start hallucinating after twenty-five hours.

10-8

Yeah, I know all about the rights criminals have in this country. But there is one right that I definitely believe in. While a criminal is in the act of committing a major crime—say a rape or an armed robbery or a murder or an attempted murder—he has the right to get capped on the spot.

10-8

If defense attorneys get the best deal in this country, crime victims get the worst. There's usually no compensation for their loss of property or loved one, no real consideration except maybe the fact that the offender gets put in jail. In some Arab countries, family members get to waste the guy who has unjustly killed one of their loved ones. Sometimes I can see that.

10-8

I know for a fact that there are lots of guys and gals whose main purpose in life is to commit crimes. They get up every day, get together, have some coffee, and make their plans for the day. I can just see it. "Well, let's rob that joint over there, then run that numbers scam over there, then bilk that old lady over there, then steal that semi full of TV sets over here, sell those drugs over there, waste this guy over here, do a little pimping over on that corner, muscle in on so-and-so's territory over there, get a piece of the action over here," and so on. That's okay, I really appreciate it. Job security, know what I mean?

10-8

There are many who oppose the death penalty. They call it inhumane, cruel and unusual punishment, a poor solution, a waste of another human life, et cetera. I'm tired of hearing about it. Let them live with, and support, the families of those who have been murdered. Let them house, feed, support, and care for the murderers, too.

10-8

I've made over 500 DUI arrests while working in a town that has no bars. You figure it out. There has to be a lot of drinking going on somewhere.

10-8

I wish we had a truth machine. One that could dig deep down, past all the lies, even past what people might erroneously think is the truth, to reach the *real* truth. No need for hearings, no need for trials. I just hook you up, and you give me the hows, the whys, and the whens. Boom! I turn you over, and you're done. No lies, no loopholes, no shows, no sympathy, just the truth. That's what I want.

10-8

The number of violent rapes reported to our department is staggeringly low. Every kind of rape is a serious crime, and, as we all learned from the Mike Tyson case, no means no. But my sympathy starts to ebb when some barfly gets blasted, goes home with some scumbag, gets raped, staggers into the PD still drunk, and can't even remember where it happened or when or how. There's an easy way to put an end to that stuff. It's called pushing away from the bar, or getting a friend or even the cops or a cab to take you home.

10-8

I once got a gun out of a car two other cops had already searched.

10-8

How do you fight crime nowadays? With computerized monitoring devices and ultra high-tech equipment that reads DNA, fingerprints, voiceprints, retinal scans, fingernail bed formations, et cetera. Obtaining such accurate and complete personal data on career criminals in the future will make it easier to match criminals with their crimes, capture, and prosecute them. Not to mention the deterrent factor when a scumbag knows his whole life is on record.

10-8

I have been known to hold a grudge. I once arrested a guy for driving with a revoked license and possession of a loaded handgun. I was new on the job, and my probable cause for the stop was really flimsy, to tell the truth. The guy walked scot free in court, but I kept my eye on him. Six years later I saw this guy stumble, and I mean stumble, out of a bar in a neighboring town while I was on-duty. I knew where he lived in my town. I raced to a particular intersection where I knew he would be passing by. At the precise moment I arrived at the intersection, I observed this guy's vehicle make a wide left turn and drive onto the grass parkway. End result: a "good" traffic stop with a Breathalyzer reading of .25, which held up in court. Justice!

10-8

There is nothing so terrible to behold as a bad divorce. What is a bad divorce? I'll tell you. It's years and years of court battles. It's the entire extended families on both sides jumping into the feud. Monstrous child-custody disputes. Piles of frustration and bickering. Physical confrontations. Young children standing by helplessly witnessing all this shit and feeling just like what they are: pawns in the game of who-can-hurt-who-the-most. In a bad divorce, no one, absolutely no one, wins. Not the parents, not the relatives, not even the attorneys, because they get sick of the whole thing.

10-8

We have traffic court once a month, every month. It's just like having a period. It's unpleasant to sit there and be stared at by all the people you pimped the month prior. Or to listen to them bicker and lie. We write little notes on the backs of our copies of the traffic ticket, describing things like weather conditions, the radar and how it was calibrated, where we were sitting at the time of the sighting of the violator, and what the violator said. I've written some very strange things on the backs of some of my tickets.

10-8

We have one supervisor who tells the biggest lies to people when they call to beef police officers. I love watching him do this. He's so smooth and fast, nobody ever suspects a thing.

10-8

Do the kids of cops and firemen and judges and prosecuting attorneys get breaks from the cops? All the time, and damn right, too!

10-8

Go ahead, make my day. While I'm writing you a speeding ticket for going 21 mph over the limit, get out of your Jeep, walk back to my squad and say, "I pay your salary. You should be looking for burglars. My Jeep was *stalling* a block before you stopped me!" Then show up in traffic court and, after a foolish attempt at a not-guilty plea, tell the judge, "I know I was speeding, but I just want you and everybody here to know that this officer was rude." Yeah, thanks, lady, thanks a lot.

10-8

Very exciting, adrenaline-pumping moment for me: waiting for the Breathalyzer to display and print out a test of .10 or more on one of my DUI arrests.

10-8

Very embarrassing moment for me: turning beet red and staring in total disbelief at an .02 reading on the Breathalyzer on one of my DUI arrests.

10-8

I just happened to be in an attorney's conference room once when this defense attorney was discussing a battery case with the prosecutor. The defense attorney said his female client hit the male victim on the head with a frying pan because she was suffering from a blood disorder. When I heard that, I started laughing and the defense attorney had me kicked out of the room. Which is okay, because five years later I got to write that defense attorney a traffic ticket in an injury car accident.

10-8

I don't know. Is it easier to just give career criminals some kind of job and pay them twenty grand a year, or to lock them up, which costs us the twenty grand anyway and serves as a breeding ground for crooks?

10-8

We have a group of guys who work over our town every few months or so. Their MO is very simple. They drive over, get out of their car, walk up to somebody else's car parked on the street or in the driveway, open the door, and take whatever they can find. Which translates into numerous police reports about missing purses, cameras, fur coats, VCRs, computers, car phones, wallets, jewelry, et cetera. Come on, folks. Get with it. Wake up to reality. *Lock your car doors.* Park your car in a *locked* garage. Best of all, don't leave anything in that car, okay?

10-8

We have several totally lost young men and women in our town who were sexually, physically, or mentally abused by their parents. These young people possess many talents and could really make a contribution. But they are held back either by what they remember or by what they don't want to remember. They're handicapped, so they turn to drugs and alcohol and crime and violence.

10-8

Public defenders have the worst job on the face of the earth. They get stuck defending absolutely the guiltiest scumbags of society all day, every day. Rapists, serial killers, you name it. The job is terrifically unpopular and the pay is not so great. Cops hate a public defender who goes all out to get an obviously guilty jerk some kind of break. But without public defenders our criminal justice system would not work. I don't like what they do, but I know somebody has to do it.

10-8

I've never yet seen a defendant go to jail for lying in court. It's like there's an unwritten rule that the defendant can lie through his teeth because everybody expects him to, because he is trying to save his own skin. But let a *cop* lie in court, and look out. I try not to lie in court. I would sooner lose a case, which I have done several times, than lie. I'm not going to blow my job or my freedom over some scum-bag.

10-8

Riots have to be scary things for cops. I have never been in one. Even the riot exercises in training scared the shit out of me. I mean, it's you against a mindless, mad mob fueled by extremely intense feelings. It's hard to predict what a mob will do, but a mob has the potential to do really chilling things that individuals would never do on their own.

10-8

If it's been raining cats and dogs and you come to a dip in the road that is filled with water and you can just make out the top of another car poking out of the water in there, please don't try to drive through, okay?

10-8

Drop guns are unregistered firearms some cops carry in case they shoot some guy who deserves it, but maybe not right then. Officially, this is an unjustified shooting incident. When this happens, the drop gun is pulled out, wiped for prints, and dropped beside the bad guy who's lying dead in some alley or something. Then the cop who shot him says, "Hey, the guy had a gun!" I don't carry a drop gun, but I think about it. I heard a story about a shooting that happened in Chicago. The evidence techs found fourteen guns in the area of this one incident. Now there's a cop who has a lot of good friends!

10-8

Almost every rookie nowadays rides around with a veteran field train-ing officer (FTO) for awhile before being cut loose on society. My FTO was a sweet, Irish guy whose father was a police sergeant and then fire chief in a nearby town. We told each other jokes for three months and had a ball. He was a good cop, a smart cop, but the administra-tion screwed him around. His ship came in when his god-uncle became head of a union and gave him a good job in the private sector. Now I see him driving around in a company car, shuffling some papers, schmoozing people, and playing golf. I'm happy to see him doing so well after quitting the PD, but I miss having him around.

10-8

One time this supervisor and a couple of our older guys wanted to gig this rookie, so they got together and hatched themselves a little plan. The supervisor called our rookie in and told him with a straight face that his girlfriend's mother had called the PD and wanted to sign a complaint against him for some kind of sex thing. The rookie had been having a few problems with his girlfriend so he took it pretty seriously, until everybody started laughing. He was really pissed. I would be, too.

10-8

Once we had a sergeant nobody liked. He was a little free about handing out suspensions, saying that it was his job. He lived in town and had this little wooden landscaping bridge in his front yard that he was very proud of. Somebody—I won't say who—swiped that sucker from his front yard while the sergeant was on-duty. Two weeks later the bridge magically appeared on the front lawn of the station, painted up like a gypsy wagon. The Sarge was on-duty at that time, too. We laughed about it for days. Somebody sure had a good time painting it.

10-8

We had this new style of holster for awhile, until we found out that convicts had devised and were practicing a move so they could disarm us and shoot us with our own gun, taken from that particular type of holster, in about a second and a half!

10-8

I've had more than 500 drunks in the back of my squad and not one has ever puked in there. That has to be some kind of record!

10-8

Phencyclidine, or PCP, is a very bad, bad drug. A person on PCP can fool you. The drug itself cycles through the brain in about fifteen-minute intervals, so you can have a guy who initially is acting a little funny but appears to be quite cooperative, and in a few seconds he becomes a madman. Contrary to popular belief, PCP does not give the user super strength. PCP is an animal tranquilizer, a downer. It can make a person absolutely impervious to pain by blocking the pain-react response. When this happens, inhuman and extraordinary things can happen, like breaking handcuffs, throwing cops around like dolls, et cetera. Very scary. One guy on PCP sliced pieces of his own face off with a piece of broken glass and fed them to his dog!

10-8

Sometimes what you learn in the police academy will serve you very well. At the academy we were taught to look out for potential weapons lying around at the scenes of domestic disputes. We saw movies and participated in many real-life simulations. Not three months after I got on the job, I was called to a domestic. We were short-handed so I was the only cop there. As I was trying to get things under control, I saw out of the corner of my eye a huge kitchen knife in the living room! You can bet I grabbed that thing right away.

10-8

Having the strongest or the biggest cop as a backup in a tight situation is not always the best when things get rough. You want the guy who instinctively does the *right thing*. That's the cop who's going to save your ass.

10-8

Things I have scrounged off the parkway while driving around in the squad: filing cabinets, bicycles, lawn furniture, a pool table, lamps, chairs, coffee tables, vacuum cleaners, a motorized tricycle, an antique railroad lantern, an antique toboggan, books, fans, typewriters, et cetera. I try to grab the stuff when it's dark out, but if it's really good stuff, I'll face the embarrassment and grab it in the daylight. I don't mind the daylight grabs because when people look out their windows and see some cop rooting around in their garbage pile, they've got to be thinking, "Poor cops still don't get paid worth a damn!"

10-8

Let's say you're a scumbag. You like being a scumbag and don't want to change. But the local police are on to you and go out of their way to pinch you so many times that they've even got a cell dedicated to you back at the PD. Hey, you've got choices. You can kill yourself, quit being a scumbag, be a scumbag only in your own room, or do the smartest and easiest thing: Get the hell outta town and be a scumbag somewhere else!

10-8

Things that cops do that you should definitely beef about: If you are a woman, one particular cop who follows you around, pulls traffic stops on you for no reason, calls you at work or at home and harasses you; cops who use excessively foul language with you; cops who use unwarranted or excessive force; cops who steal or try to squeeze you for protection; cops who sell dope. There are thousands and thousands of cops around. There are bound to be a few bad apples, and for some reason, they're still on the street. It only takes one bad cop, or one bad act by a cop, to put an entire police force to shame in front of John Q. Public.

10-8

After every staff meeting, we're always told the same thing: more enforcement, wear your hat at all times, call out your traffic stops. It's the same thing every time. And this has been going on for years.

10-8

Cat burglars are unusual in that they enter homes and steal stuff at night while the people are at home, in bed. Pretty bold, if you ask me. We had a cat burglar who was not very smart working our town. He always worked the same area and used the same MO. He'd drive to the scene in the early morning hours and park his ride in somebody's driveway. Then he would slip into houses with unlocked doors or windows and take stuff like purses and cameras. He would even take pictures of the people while they were asleep! He got caught when he locked himself out of his car one morning and asked a neighbor for a hammer so he could break out a window. The astute neighbor called the cops and we grabbed the suspect with some of the goods. The car was stolen, too.

10-8

Ask me if I believe in the existence of evil. I've been on enough crime scenes, suicide scenes, and forced-entry burglaries to know that if evil doesn't permanently inhabit, at the very least it visits the minds of men. On a bad crime scene, especially a residential burglary, I can feel the intensity of the intent to do an evil thing. Evil thoughts abounded in the planning and the execution of that crime. I can see it in the broken locks, the looted drawers. Suicides and murders are bad, because a very great crime has been committed: the premeditated killing of a human being. At the scenes of suicides I get the feeling that evil has visited, even if only for a moment, long enough to take a life. Yes, I believe in the existence of evil, and yes, it scares me.

10-8

Eating spicy foods on midnights is not a good idea. Your digestive tract is already reeling from dining at those odd hours, like at 3:00 in the morning. You throw some spicy food in there, and you are going to pay, big time.

10-8

When you're out there driving around in your heap and it looks like it's going to go nose up, please drive it off the roadway first so you don't block traffic, okay? That is what the shoulder of the highway is for. Don't choose to have the vehicle die in our busiest intersection and make life miserable for me and everybody else.

10-8

Over half of my hand tools I have found lying on the road while I was on-duty, and that includes large pipe wrenches!

10-8

Nowadays we can only shoot somebody if they are going to kill somebody or cause great bodily harm. I guess it makes sense. In the bygone days, cops could pop somebody for doing lots of things, like arson, rape, burglary, and stuff. Times have changed.

10-8

A guy with a knife fifteen feet away can charge and stab you before you can pull your gun out of its holster and fire off a round. Think about how far away that is when you're dealing with people.

10-8

Lots of cops get killed with their own service weapons. I could be killed with the same gun I wear to protect myself and others.

10-8

How about this? Cops are getting better at their jobs. More and more people are turning to crime because of drugs. Our jails are extremely overcrowded. Why not take ten guys who have committed a similar crime and put them on a work team? House them together, give them jobs together, and pay them together. Let them do government work or ecological cleanup or inner-city projects. One rule: If one or some of the guys walk away, when they get caught they get put in a room for five minutes with the guys they left behind, who have to go back to jail for five more years with no parole!

10-8

We once had a rookie cop who, by accident, totally cornered this cat burglar in a yard not far from where a burglary had been called out. Our man was so excited when he raised his shotgun to his shoulder that he forgot he had his portable radio in his left hand, with the On button pushed down. The rookie was shouting at the poor perp, "Get down, motherfucker! Get fucking down!" He said it over and over and everybody heard it. It was even on tape. His nickname is Potty Mouth.

10-8

It took me eight months to get hired for the cop job. In between, I was driving a limo and working construction. The day I got my hire letter, I went out into the backyard and screamed. I must have known what was coming.

10-8

There are certain traffic signs posted in my town which I believe are wrong. I absolutely will not enforce those signs because, as a civilian, I would disregard them.

10-8

There's this tough town not far from us. I went to the PD there on a case. They had this holding cell in their station that was essentially an animal cage. There was a naked, foaming-at-the-mouth guy hanging from the ceiling of the cage like a monkey. Great town.

10-8

Almost every time I tell a guy he will get a signature bond from the judge at bond court, he gets a cash bond which he can't post and he gets locked up. Oh, well.

10-8

When I go to bond court, I look in the bullpen and stare at our society's failures straight in the face. Murderers are sitting next to forgers, drunk vagrants next to drug dealers, burglars next to wife-beaters, and on and on it goes. As their names are called, each person steps forward to tell his story to the judge. That story usually contains a pinch of poverty, a bit of abuse, or a rash of violence. But always there is an underlying lack of love and dignity. Bond court is just another cog in the court machine, a machine made up of humans processing other humans day after day, hour after hour, year after year.

10-8

Once there were these two bad guys who were desperate, to say the least. One guy walked into our Kmart, filled a shopping cart to the brim with clothes, and just wheeled that sucker right out the front door, without paying, of course. His buddy, the wheelman, was waiting curbside with the getaway vehicle, a blue Chevy Caprice with no plates. Store security got a description of the vehicle, which was dispatched immediately on an area-wide band. Upshot: Two hours later our men were pinched in a wealthy suburb not too far away. The observant arresting officer saw the car and occupants matching our broadcast—not to mention the clothes piled up so high in the back seat that they were plainly visible from Timbuktu. Why didn't our thieves stop and put the clothes in the trunk? Because it was already filled up with stolen tires from a local Shell station.

10-8

We have this one intersection on the south side of town that is a total mess. Way too much traffic at rush hour and on Saturdays. And there is a railroad freight line conveniently located right there, too. I always get sent down there on calls, and then I get stuck in traffic. Real bummer. But what can I do? I get sent, I gotta go.

10-8

One time we had this construction project going on at the freight tracks just east of the highway that runs through our town. These foreigners drive right through this maze of sixteen construction barricades and a few ROAD BLOCKED DO NOT ENTER signs, and get stuck on the tracks. So, of course, a freight train comes along and sweeps their clunker all the way to China. And they tried to sue the city. Hell, they should feel lucky they weren't in the car when it got hit!

10-8

Getting a search warrant is like giving birth. First, you have to scrape up good probable cause and present it to a state's attorney. He has to review it and then grant you a warrant, which must be written up and then typed by a secretary. The areas to be searched and the descriptions of what you're looking for must be very specifically stated in the warrant. Then you, the cop, have to walk it over to a courtroom and try to get the warrant in front of a judge. Then he looks it over, asks you a few questions, decides if your warrant is okay, and determines how long you have to execute it (usually no longer than three days). Then you have to take the warrant to the county clerk's office to get your baby registered. Then you have to execute the warrant in the specified time period. And whether you do or not, you have to take that thing back to the judge who granted it in the first place, and tell him what happened. Only then is your search warrant finally, finally, laid to rest. Like I said, getting a search warrant is like having a baby.

10-8

I've arrested easily more than 1,200 people, and not one has taken a pop at me. I'm way, way overdue to eat lunch. But that's okay. When it happens, I'll just take it and call for backup.

10-8

Cops don't generally like to work the dispatcher desk because you're stuck in a little room all day listening to people bitch about the water in their basement or their neighbor's dog, and the supervisors are everywhere, looking over your shoulder. The only good thing about working the desk is that sometimes you can pretend you are a supervisor and totally punt some citizen's beef about you or some other copper in your department. I love doing that.

10-8

Most cops hate court because the time and date are almost always scheduled for the convenience of the offender, the offender's attorney, the judge, anybody but the cop. There's nothing like facing up to a grueling cross-examination by some dork defense attorney about a case that's more than a year old, after a midnight shift, when you've been awake more than twenty-four hours.

10-8

Let's say you get a traffic ticket in this one town, but you know a cop real well in the next town. You can try calling your buddy, but usually the best thing you can hope for is supervision on that ticket. Cops cannot usually make tickets just disappear.

10-8

Once these people we knew real well in our town tried to report a hit-and-run accident on one of their cars. When I got to the house they took me right away to the "scene." The driver's side mirror of their vehicle supposedly had been smashed by a passing car while it was parked in the driveway. I could see pieces of the mirror had been nicely laid on the driveway right below the broken mirror. There was only one problem. The car was parked with the damaged side so close to the side of garage that even a bicyclist couldn't have gotten through, an obvious setup. I gave them an insurance note on it, stating that the accident happened at an unknown location at an unknown time.

10-8

I once stopped this guy for a minor traffic offense. The car came back reported stolen, but I knew he was the registered owner because he had all kinds of ID, including a military ID from a nearby base. It turns out the bank that had loaned him the money for the car had reported the vehicle as stolen and put a lien on it. I just let the guy go. I hate banks.

10-8

I can always tell when someone I've stopped for a traffic offense lives in a bad neighborhood. Their trunk lock is usually punched out. They're carrying things like long pipes, baseball bats, kitchen knives, nunchuks, broom handles, you name it. But I don't do anything, because I can understand why they have those things in their cars.

10-8

There are guys in our town who drive cars that are worth two to three times a cop's annual salary. That's pretty disgusting is what it is. But hey, if it wasn't for rich people, who would we poor people work for?

10-8

Here's a good story. Once I was given this "mandate" by some friends to "get" this one guy because he was being a jerk about a divorce. So I see this guy a few days later and pull him over for a vehicle violation. Well, it turns out that this guy is suspended so I arrest him for it, book him, and then release him on bond. It's right at the end of shift, so as I'm driving home at 10:00 o'clock at night I see the guy walking home. He lived far away, and it was winter, so I decided to be nice and offer this guy a ride. He doesn't recognize me (most civilians don't recognize cops out of uniform), but he gets in my car anyway. Not three blocks down the road, I get pulled over by a copper I know real well from the next town over. I was going maybe 7 miles over the speed limit. The copper walks up to my car, recognizes me right away, and we have a little chat. The cop then walks back to his squad, and we drive on. Now my passenger is looking at me like I'm God or something. He starts in on how all cops are jerks and how he just got arrested by one, and he's saying that I must have some pull because the cop didn't even ask me for my license. To make a long story short, the guy didn't figure out who I was until we were two blocks from his house and I said his address! What a sap.

10-8

Please don't say, "You can't give me a ticket!" and then drive away from a cop on a traffic stop. Very bad move. You will get the ticket, plus some others that might include fleeing and eluding and failure to obey the direction of a police officer. People do this, though, every once in a while.

10-8

Once in evidence technician school, I was shown a slide of a gal who had been shot six times in the driveway of her home. She was killed by her jealous husband, who happened to be a cop. She was very good-looking. About five of the six shots appeared to have been fatal. Believe me, when we want to waste somebody, we know how to do it, even if that somebody is a loved one.

10-8

How many cops does it take on the local force to make your life miserable? Just one.

10-8

Off-duty, I once spotted this feisty gal copper from the next town running radar patrol. I had an older personal car at the time, and I wanted to "test" her a little bit. Even though I was in traffic, I knew she would be paying particular attention to my car, because beaters are cop-attention magnets in the suburbs, so I drove past her going maybe 6 or 7 mph over the posted speed limit. She waited awhile but then, sure enough, she pulled out after I was already two blocks away. I sped up a little. Then she sped up a little. So I sped up a little more. Pretty soon she realized she was going 60 mph and not getting any closer to my car. So she flipped her overheads on. But I was right by my police station so I ducked into the parking lot real quick. When she pulled in behind me, I called her by name and said I was late for work. She was snotty about it and said something about some copper leading her on a chase. And she told me not to do it in her town. That night I caught a DUI that she and her fellow coppers had been chasing around for an hour.

10-8

One Sunday morning I stopped this guy from Wisconsin for speeding on the highway. The guy said he'd left his driver's license at home, and gave me a name and date of birth. That information came back "no record," so I arrested the guy and took him to the station. I knew he was lying and locked him up right away. I did get his home phone number in Milwaukee first, though. I called his home and pretended I was from the Illinois State Lottery. I used the name of a passenger that was in my guy's car and said that this guy had purchased a winning lottery ticket for the name my arrestee had given me. At that point the woman who answered the phone said that so-and-so was only one and a half years old. I said, "I'm sorry, you have to be over eighteen to collect," and hung up. Then I went back to the guy in the cell and gave him hell. It turned out the guy had a revoked driver's license and had given me his son's name.

10-8

Once this rookie and his FTO from our department arrested this German guy, who'd tried to flee and elude, for DUI. The guy was being a real jerk at the station and said he never drank. He was such a jerk that we ended up wrestling with him. His wallet fell on the floor. In it, we found pictures of him from his last vacation in Hawaii, including one of these hula dancers mixing a party margarita in this guy's mouth!

10-8

One time this state trooper stopped this guy for traffic a bit north of our town. The guy had a suspended driver's license but the trooper felt sorry for him so he not only let the guy go, he gave the guy a ride to the train station so the guy could go home. Well, the car the guy was driving turned out to be stolen. So the shift commander and I got sent to our train station to wait for this guy. We thought we would have a problem identifying the guy, but it was late at night and the train only had one car in use with only three passengers. One was a fiftyish businesswoman. The other was an older businessman. That left one really skanky-looking dude who tried to slide down in his seat upon our approach. We yanked this perp off the train and took him to our station. The guy was a nut. He'd seen the car that he'd stolen running at the curb in front of a courthouse and tried to get in to take it for a ride. Then this guy started telling me about an armed robbery he did and how he has mental problems and suicidal tendencies. Soon the state trooper showed up. I couldn't help but notice that his squad had no prisoner partition. So here I made a slight blunder. I told the trooper, right in front of our offender, that the guy had suicidal tendencies. As soon as I said that the guy got a funny look in his eye. He jumped up and ran over to another table a few feet away. He reached down and grabbed a telephone cable wire, put it around his neck, and began to "strangle" himself. The trooper and I just stood there looking at this dope. Finally I said, "Hey fella, if you wanna kill yourself you're going to have to try some other way to do it."

10-8

We've had two union votes in the last six years at our PD. The last vote was 22 to 19 against the union. That means that there are some pretty unhappy campers at our department.

10-8

The squads we drive around now are the best. They're the "bathtub" Chevy Caprices with antilock brakes, air bag, air conditioning, and a responsive fuel-injected 350 engine. They're safe, maneuverable, and zippy. The hubcaps have a tendency to fly off, and the windshield is raked back at such a radical angle that the wind whistles over the overhead light bar at higher speeds. And the dashboard top, which is very deep because of the raked windshield, is curved at the edge, so we can't put drinks and burgers and stuff on it. Otherwise, they're great cars.

10-8

Let me say this: Kids and alcohol do not mix. I'll say it again: *Kids and alcohol do not mix.* As a matter of fact, some adults and alcohol don't mix!

10-8

We had this guy named John who was a regular customer of ours for a time. Once he burglarized his girlfriend's apartment at about 8:30 at night. We all knew he didn't have a driver's license or a car so we just hid out by the train station. Sure enough, John showed up faithfully for the 9:10 train. He didn't make it to the train, though. He spent the night in our "Graybar Hotel."

10-8

Cops, as a rule, don't like the dark. We know that a lot of criminals reserve the time after sunset and before sunrise for some of their best work; projects like burglaries to autos, sexual assaults, non-residential burglaries, drug deals, arsons, vandalisms, murders, et cetera. As cops, we like the light to keep the bad guys away and to keep the truth out in the open where we can see it.

10-8

I've strained my back several times trying to upright bent street sign posts after they've been run over by idiot drunk motorists (who somehow managed afterwards to still get the car home in the barn), just to avoid taking the paper on a hit-and-run accident.

10-8

Some things I check every day when I get in my squad: the gas gauge, the spotlight, the overhead lights, the shotgun, the mirrors, and underneath the back seat.

10-8

There's this one little piece of property located at precisely that point on this one road where lots of people like to fly off into the bushes. The landowner got so tired of having to re-plant bushes and trees that he paid big money to put huge rocks the size of Gibraltar there. I don't want to be around when the next person drives off the road and smacks one of those babies. No way.

10-8

We have vast, untapped human resources in our country. We have a few huge problems in our country. Why not apply those vast untapped resources to some of those problems? *Convicts* represent a huge segment of unused resources. They now get free room and board at our expense. We pay about $20,000 per year, per inmate, just so these people can make absolutely no contribution. In fact, when convicts get out, they usually make a negative contribution. While in prison, they are disenfranchised, kept ignorant, schooled to do new crimes, and are generally pissed off. In essence, our prisoners are being trained to become better criminals at the expense of the taxpayer. This is wrong. It's just like the welfare thing. You can't throw money at people and expect them to have any dignity or self-worth. So what if you took inmates and applied them to tasks such as ecological cleanup or inner-city cleanup? For that matter, what if you took the elderly and people on welfare and gave them jobs doing the same thing? With a regular paycheck, given in exchange for a contribution to society, comes dignity. Just a thought.

10-8

Bank employees are trained to hand over a specified sum of cash during armed robberies. I don't like this. I think bank employees should be weapons-trained and have loaded guns within reach at work. This may sound crazy, but it's cheaper to buy a few guns than to fork over $2,500 in cash a few times. Or how about this? Give bank robbers poisoned cash, so as soon as they handle it they die, or use cash that has a chemical on it that dissolves it after a short time in contact with air. Sounds rather radical, but so are bank robbers.

10-8

So you don't know exactly what happened, but you've been raped. Come right to us. Do not wash or clean up. Preserve any evidence. Try to get a good description of the jerk fixed in your mind, including identifying marks. Get vehicle descriptions, plates, times, places. Be prepared to face surly, unsympathetic cops, doctors, nurses, husbands, relatives, friends and slick, scumbag, defense attorneys who will not hesitate to peel your personal life open like a can of sardines in front of the entire world. It sounds like a rough row to hoe. But even rougher is what could happen to the next person who gets raped by the guy who did you. You maybe could prevent it by taking the guy to court. And it may help you to deal with your ordeal if you help us nail the bastard.

10-8

Hey, you businesses, it's the Information Age, right? Why don't you network together to help detect shoplifters, robbers, and bad check writers? Get faxed posters circulated and pinned up right by those cash registers. Let the criminal jerks take a gander at their own mugs when they try to do your store. Be on the ball and broadcast crime info messages to all the other stores in your area or franchise network. Come on, you can do it! Help the cops by helping yourselves.

10-8

Gambling. Have I got a problem with that, or what? To me, gambling is only a crime when people are being ripped off by crooked gamers or being charged ridiculously unlawful interest on gambling debts. Guys want to throw some dice, lay off a few bets on a game, or play a little poker, it's okay with me. Right now we've got Las Vegas and Atlantic City, church bingo and casino nights, riverboat gambling, carnivals, and the lotteries, and they're all legal. Now running your own casino might be a little out of hand, unless, of course, jobs were created and the government got its cut. Awarding gambling franchises to the American Indians, like in Wisconsin? I don't know. We owe them something, though. A lot of people think gambling of any kind is wrong. Unfortunately for them, gambling is here to stay. Hey, life itself is a gamble in a lot of ways.

10-8

Shop owners, please, and I mean *please*, do *not* put your most expensive, most portable items on open display in the front window or by the front door! Furriers and leather shops, keep those expensive coats on secured cables, okay? At least turn every other coat hanger the other way, to discourage big grabs off the rack. You don't want to be staring at empty hangers while dumbly scratching your head at the end of the day. Electronics stores, you can bolt down your display items, or cable them, too. That won't bother me. Really.

10-8

A big, big major, major crime in our country is cheating on your income taxes. Everybody does it, either illegally by under-reporting or legally through a phalanx of accountants, tax attorneys, and piles of paperwork. I say we cut the bullshit and the IRS. Just have the government yank 10% of everybody's incoming loot right away. Forget about exemptions, forget about complicated forms and tax rules, forget about filing, forget about April 15, and forget about the IRS. Go ahead, make it 12% or even more if you have to. But God only asks for 10%, so why should the government get more?

10-8

Quick-change artists are fun to watch, and the good ones are not easy to catch. They can scam anybody running a cash register out of hundreds of dollars in about three minutes. Be very suspicious of anyone who requests more than two "Can-I-have-change?" transactions.

10-8

My solutions to dealing with repeat sexual offenders may seem a bit drastic. Lobotomize, castrate, or drug the suckers senseless. Or just pile them all together in one place and let them molest each other! Locking them up in jail and then cutting them loose on society does not seem like a real good idea to me.

10-8

Message to the women of the world: Until things get better, you're going to have to *assert* yourselves a little bit for your own survival. Learn self-defense. You'd be surprised at what you are capable of doing when your life is on the line. I'm talking keys, pepper spray, whistles, elbows, knees, teeth, screaming, spitting, biting, scratching, socking, slashing, guns, knives, hatpins.... I'm getting scared just writing this. A criminal's size and strength mean nothing when met with readiness and training. Try like hell not to get into situations that are conducive to things like purse-snatching, date rape, or sexual assaults. And stay away from potentially abusive situations.

10-8

Look really close at Mr. Smooth-talking-stranger-in-a-suit who offers you whopping interest or returns on certain "investments." It only takes a few phone calls to check this guy out to see if he's legit. You don't have to be paranoid about it, but it's *your* money so what's the harm in getting some references and doing a little checking around before forking over your hard-earned cash to a stranger?

10-8

We had a guy in our town who lost his wife and child to a relatively minor house fire. They were found dead of smoke inhalation, huddled under the window of a second-story bedroom. The guy had the whole house torn down. For years the land, which was in a prime area, remained vacant. Now there's a new house there.

10-8

Career criminals beware: Your time is up. You are going to become the first casualties of the Information Age. We will encumber you with software and hardware, knowing that there is close to a 100% chance that you will keep committing crimes. We will simply follow you around or monitor you until you do. And then you'll be caught and baked, turn you over, you're done!

10-8

I once got an owl call. These people called and said there was an owl in their bathroom. I went there expecting to see this ferocious, huge, horned owl. Instead it was a baby screech owl perched quietly on the shower curtain rod. I threw a towel over it and took it outside.

10-8

Another time I chased a baby squirrel around the utility room of some-body's basement for an hour before I caught it in a laundry basket! Think about it, a cop chasing around a squirrel, for God's sake.

10-8

A lot of a cop's time is spent on overt patrol, which translates into that high-profile, uniform-flashing, gun-toting, marked-squad, driving-around kind of thing. This show of force actually does work in some instances. But we can't be everywhere. You people are going to have to handle *most* of the crime prevention load yourselves. How do you do that? Simple. Use common sense. Lock up your valuables or spread out your losses by keeping some of the good stuff here, some over there, et cetera. Stay away from bad neighborhoods. Stay away from bad people. Try like hell not to find yourself alone, unarmed, in high-risk situations. Learn self-defense. Learn about criminals. Stay away from drugs and the people who sell them. Do not try to play Joe Cop yourself unless you have to; doing so can lead to all sorts of trouble, unless you know you have an edge. Know the cop lingo in your area for easier reporting. Unfortunately, cops in towns right next to each other might possess a stunning array of different, baffling codes which are confusing and unnecessary. As a business person, keep an eye on three things: register receipts, inventory, and your own employees. More goods get swiped out the back door by employees than out the front by thieves and shoplifters. Watch the layout of your retail store. Keep that cash register somewhere near, but not too close to, the front door, so customers have to pass it to leave your store. A number-one way to reduce shoplifting is to have your employees greet each customer by looking them in the eye and saying to their face, "Can I help you?" Use good locks and bars and alarms. Have your employees learn how to spot shoplifters and to describe criminals. Get license plates, but don't take undue risks. And remember, *common sense* is the first line of defense when it comes to stopping crime.

10-8

Parents: *Keep an eye on your kids.* Look for strange changes in behavior and strange new friends, late hours, and heaps of TVs, VCRs, bicycles, stereos, and cash piling up suddenly in your garage or your kid's room. This might tell you something.

10-8

One time I got sent on a mouse-in-the-house call. So I get to the house, and the breathless twelve-year-old daughter answers the door and says, "My mom has it trapped in the bedroom closet!" I go in there, and Mom has a broom pushed up against the back wall of the closet. "I got it cornered!" she says. So I tell her to relax, and I get down there on the floor to have a look-see. The culprit is a field mouse the size of a dime, and it's dead from fright. I did my duty and took care of the body.

10-8

One time I got dispatched on a well-being check in a mansion by the lake. The homeowners were in Europe, and the maid who worked there had not called or come home for some hours. I rang the doorbell and got no answer, so I walked around the house and looked through the window into the kitchen. I saw feet lying on the kitchen floor. I got in through an open back door and found the maid dead of a heart attack. I notified the coroner and had the dispatcher call the relatives. The coroner came, he and I put the body in a body bag, and he took it away. I left a note for the homeowners.

10-8

Almost every cop has a pet peeve, something that really gets him or her riled. It could be child abuse, armed robbery, homicide, even just speeding. With me, it's drunk drivers. If you're drunk and driving, you don't want to be around me when I'm on-duty because I will do everything in my power to find you, peel you out of your car, arrest you, yank your precious driver's license, and put you on a bicycle!

10-8

When I had about a year on, one of our coppers got killed in the line of duty. He was hit by a box truck at night. The truck driver fell asleep and hit our officer, who was out of his squad car by the highway, working the stop of a vehicle that matched a description from a felony. The box truck plowed into three squad cars and the stopped vehicle. Our man was thrown for many feet and died instantly. I was called in to guard the accident scene. It was eerie, sitting there in a squad car on the highway looking at this guy's boot here, his hat over there, his gun over there, and squad cars all tossed around. Rob had ten years on the job, was married, and was one of the nicest, smartest cops we had. As if that wasn't bad enough, the felony call he'd stopped the car for was bogus. A kid called in a fake attempted burglary and gave a false vehicle description to impress the lady who lived across the street.

10-8

We had this cop named Lester, who had been on for a long time and was pretty fed up with animal calls. One day he gets this call of suspicious noises in the walls at this house. He goes over and tries to schmooz this frantic gal about it, but she's not having any of it and says, "I want you to do something about this right now!" So Lester goes out to his squad car, gets his shotgun, brings it in the house, racks in a round, and points it at the wall where the noises were coming from. The lady changed her mind and told Lester she'd call an exterminator.

10-8

Here's another Lester story. Lester had a reputation for being the world's best punter. Once I got called to the scene of a hit-and-run accident on private property, with an assault-and-battery thrown in. It was right near the end of the shift, and I was staring some serious, unwanted overtime in the face. Lester showed up and put his arms around these two guys who had punched each other out over this accident thing and said, "Hey look, we take this report and we're gonna have to charge you guys and you guys are friends and you'll have to go to court" and blah, blah, blah. End result: The guys wanted to work it out between themselves, no complaints or reports to be made. Thank you, Lester!

10-8

One time I stopped this guy for a traffic violation and then arrested him on a warrant out of Chicago. As I was getting ready to lock him up, I told him to take off his shoes. When he did, I noticed ten little packets of powder in one shoe. I'd already read him his rights so I asked him straight out what the stuff was. He said it was heroin. That got him a year in jail.

10-8

One time I had this big guy out on the side of the highway on a traffic stop, and he challenged me. So I said, "Okay, here's what we'll do. I will call for backup. And then you and me and four other guys can wrestle down in this ditch here, and I guarantee you are going to lose." He still wouldn't submit. So I called for backup. Just one other copper showed up. As soon as he did, the big guy meekly handed that cop his car keys and submitted to the stop. I arrested him for suspended driver's license.

10-8

My buddy Lester once got sent on an "annoying bird" call. This crow was diving on kids in this one neighborhood. Lester arrived, assessed the situation, took out his shotgun and promptly blasted the offender out of the sky. Well, it turns out that it was some kid's pet crow, and they call the station in a huff and ask for the body. Lester, forever on the ball, gets on the phone and says, "I'm sorry, but we gave it a state burial!" What he really did was throw the body in the landfill.

10-8

Lester and I once got sent to this house on a domestic. We'd been there several times before. The old lady was short, squat, ugly, and nasty, and had been kicked out of the house and was living in an apartment. But she wanted the only garage-door opener to the house, even though she didn't live there. The husband, of slight build, took me to their bedroom and showed me where his old lady had run right through the locked door, busting out the frame, on an earlier occasion. So we were telling the lady to leave, and to leave the garage door opener, but she wouldn't leave. I was new on the job and so I was saying right in front of her, while she's planted herself in a living room chair, "Lester, let's arrest her. Let's bust her. She won't do what the cops are telling her to do!" But Lester was being real nice, getting her a drink, talking to her, letting her phone her lawyer, and stuff. We left without doing anything. And a couple of days later, the lady beefed Lester!

10-8

I always try to keep a very low profile when I go on calls. That gives me plenty of room to elevate my authority a step or two should the situation demand it, with culmination being an arrest, if need be. This has worked very well for me over the years. The times I've gone in mad, well, they didn't work out so well. When you arrive on a call and you're already angry and shouting, there's only one place to go from there: arrest.

10-8

I've never taken a bribe. I think it's funny when motorists offer me ten or twenty or even fifty bucks to get out of a ticket. I just say, "I appreciate your offer. But I can't blow forty grand a year for twenty bucks."

10-8

Today, eighty-six men, women, and children died needlessly because they were caught up by the whims of a religious fanatic. Religion will always be with us, and thus so will religious fanatics. Which is okay, until the point these individuals decide they are God and then try to play God. They use their personal charm or charisma or whatever they can to get a hold on and twist others beyond reason, beyond hope, and beyond love. When these fanatics eventually see that they are losing control and that maybe they aren't God, they crash, and they almost always take as many people with them as they can. Then we're left sifting among the debris, wondering how we could have prevented one more apocalypse.

10-8

One time, at 4:30 in the morning, I got called in to work a traffic control detail at a bad accident on the highway. We used to have this intersection at the south end of town that stopped both highway cars and cross traffic. It was the first stoplight a motorist might encounter, coming up all the way from Florida on this particular highway. It was dark there and motorists would be heading north and people would just fall asleep at the wheel and rear-end other motorists stopped at this light. I remember it was January, the coldest day of the year. A loaded fuel tanker stopped at the stoplight was rear-ended by another semi. There was a Mustang with three people in it stopped next to the fuel tanker at the time of the collision. Final tally: striking semi driver dead and two out of the three people in the Mustang dead. The fire was so hot, a traffic light pole melted down like a candle. Ten people died at that intersection in the first six years I was on the PD. Finally they got smart and made it into an overpass. There's only been one fatality in that area in the past four years.

10-8

What does a cop do when he loses what he thought was an airtight case because of a wrong word or a technicality or a loophole and a scumbag walks? We eat it, learn from it, and go on.

10-8

There is a tremendous amount of politics in our department. In every police department, actually. It took me years to figure it out because I guess I'm just stupid that way. I wish I had known about politics a little earlier in my career.

10-8

Our current chief is big into physical fitness, which is not so bad. But now we have to have a physical fitness assessment every year, whether we need one or not. It's like a mini-Olympics and I'm always totally exhausted afterwards. We never had to do this stuff before. I wonder if it's really helping us out. Only time will tell.

10-8

Seat belts are great. They can save someone's life, or at the very least, his face. I wear a seat belt in my personal car, but not while I'm driving around in the squad. It covers my gun and gets my uniform dirty,

and I'm worried about having to jump out of the car quickly. And yet
I know I should wear one.

10-8

Twice I've had other motorists strike my parked squad while I was
handling another car accident. Not good, not good at all.

10-8

Gypsies have one other thing going for them besides being far more
organized than the police. Some of them have magic. Many times we
get calls about a theft where there were eight to ten gypsies driving
around in a large old truck, with cloth sides painted pink, orange, and
green. We rush over to the area, and we never see them. It's like they
just evaporate. Only once did I catch any; six in a beater Chevy implicated in the theft of $600 from the cash register of a restaurant in our
town. I say implicated because even though they had the dough on
them, they walked on the case because no one actually saw who
dipped into the cash register! They gave up the money as restitution,
though, but that's because we contaminated the money in their eyes,
by touching it!

10-8

I wish some black people could understand where cops are coming
from. Many blacks harbor a deep resentment for the police, especially white cops, probably due to the way they've been treated in the
past. They feel we're just another cog in the great white-run, black-
stomping machine that continues to push them down. What black people don't understand is that cops are people, too. We form our opinions from what we see and what we have to deal with on a day-to-day
basis on the job. Imagine a new white cop on the job. He's immersed
in hideous, unending, black-on-black crime, day after day. He has to
wade among ignorance, hatred, and fear on a constant basis. After a-
while, how do you think he's going to feel?

10-8

Child abuse is about as low as you can go. Even in my nice little town,
kids die from it. And what about the kids who live? They're likely to

perpetuate the abuse, keep it going for another generation.

10-8

I've arrested big executives for IBM, all they way down to guys with just the clothes on their backs.

10-8

A good drunk can fool you out on the road. After all, it isn't that hard to keep that car pointed straight ahead if you concentrate real hard, until you need your reflexes for a quick decision, such as avoiding another motorist or an obstruction or adjusting for bad road conditions. Then you're going to make a mistake, and you're going to pay me a little visit down at the PD. If you don't kill yourself or somebody else first.

10-8

When I was in Breathalyzer school, during a controlled testing session I pounded down eight beers in less that two hours and only blew an .11, which is just slightly over the legal limit. And I had a good buzz on. How much does a guy have to drink to blow .20 and .30 or more? I just can't comprehend it. It's sick how much people drink and then get behind the wheel.

10-8

Once I was in the state's attorney's office getting a warrant when I noticed some color photos in a pile on a window sill. I started casually flipping through them. They were photos of several homicides. In one, a sailor stabbed another sailor right through the heart with a butcher knife after he found out the guy was doing his girlfriend. In another, a black man shot another black man through the heart with a .45 in a bar. The guy's defense was, "I thought the other guy had a gun." Death can come quickly.

10-8

Once I went down to the Chicago police headquarters' lockup to pick up a guy on one of my warrants. On my way up to the tenth floor the elevator stopped and opened at several of the floors and I would catch a glimpse just of fingers poking through a cage, or something. It was spooky.

10-8

You may have heard stories about bushes and trees going 60 or 70 mph on radar. Well, I'm here to tell you it's true. There's a bush on my patrol that sometimes gives me a 55 reading. There used to be a tree that gave me a 45 when the wind was blowing. It's kind of a mystery why they do that. That's all I can say. I can't work radar where that's happening.

10-8

How can you fool the radar? Have a low, wedge-shaped car or drive beside a semi all the time. The larger object's profile will almost always be the one that registers on the radar gun.

10-8

For ten years they've let me carry a gun and a baton around on the job. That's awesome, totally awesome when you think about it. I have the power to save a life or to take a life. That's scary.

10-8

Once after I had eight years on the job, I took a sergeant's test that was so hard we thought it was the lieutenant's test! Twenty-seven guys took it. Only three passed and there were three openings for sergeant at the time. I got the second-highest grade. They only filled one opening, the guy that got the *lowest* passing grade. Me and the guy who got the highest scores on the test somehow flunked an oral exam which we had both passed four years earlier, when we had less time on and less training. No explanations were given.

10-8

I would have made a great defense attorney. But I would always harbor one great fear: What if I got some client off on a murder charge or something and then that person went out and killed somebody else?

10-8

Some people *use* the police in a divorce. They lie, they whine, they make up stuff, all to make their spouses look bad. I'll swear, some of them are getting coached by their attorneys or by bitter friends who have played the game and lost. We had one couple that actually would race to the front lobby of the PD so each could be the first to file a complaint on the other. Cops have their own problems, for God's sake. We don't need other people's dirty laundry shoved in our faces just because they're bitter and greedy!

10-8

Let's say I go on some call, or I'm on a traffic stop, and I find myself immediately embroiled in an argument with some jerk. What do I do? I call over my supervisor. That's what they're for. Sometimes that's all a situation needs. People will listen to a white shirt and a gold badge and some stripes, no matter what the supervisor has to say, whether it makes sense or not.

10-8

One of our deputy chiefs made chief. We had mandatory stress tests for city employees over fifty years old, and this guy, although he looked fabulous, had a history of heart problems. So they're giving him this stress test and it's near the end and they're encouraging him on a little. There was another city worker waiting for his test and he heard, "Come on, you're almost done, you can do it, come on...CODE BLUE, CODE BLUE!" I'm sorry to say the chief didn't survive bypass surgery. He was a nice guy and could tell a joke better than anyone I know.

10-8

I hate to hear that so-and-so committed some crime because he was drunk or on drugs or because he's retarded, like it wasn't his fault. Bullshit. Unless somebody's holding a gun to your head, ultimately *you* and *you alone* should be responsible for what you choose to do!

10-8

I live and work on an asphalt slab, a megalopolis jungle that stretches for hundreds of miles from Indiana through Illinois up to Wisconsin and Upper Michigan. Thousands and thousands of strip shopping centers, fast-food restaurants, car dealerships, banks, businesses, factories, stores, houses, apartments, condos. It's endless, just endless. And cold.

10-8

I'm not sure I'd like to be a judge. Stuck behind the big bench meting out life-or-death decisions all day, every day, has to be rough sometimes. And what about divorce court? Who wants to hear all that? The bitterness in that court permeates the walls, the benches, the clients, the judges, the bailiffs, even the attorneys.

10-8

To get hired, I had to take a written test, a physical-fitness test, a swim test, a lie-detector test, a psych test, an oral exam, and a physical exam. Our department can afford to be very picky. Many hundreds of people apply for maybe one, two, or at most, three positions. You'd think we'd end up with super men and women. Sometimes we do, sometimes we don't. And no one has come up with a test to really smoke out that "crazy" gene.

10-8

I was thirty years old when I became a cop. The other two guys I came on with were twenty-three and twenty-four. Four hundred and fifty people applied for three jobs. I got the last opening.

10-8

I go to bond court a lot. When I do, I always eyeball the bullpen to see who is in there. I see about 70% black, about 15% Hispanic, and about 15% white. Don't everybody get upset, that's just what I see in there.

10-8

So you're trying to become a cop and you think you've passed all your tests. The powers that be assign you a percentage score somewhere between 70 and 100, and rank you on a final list. Then the PD starts to hire from the top of the list. But they can skip people to reach for those they want. Like if somebody has a connection, like their father is chief of police.

10-8

Once in awhile one of our many stoplights will malfunction. It'll show red in all directions, which is not so bad, or green in all directions, which is a disaster...or the lights might go out completely, like during a power outage. So we have to get out of the car and direct traffic. This is always risky, because one car out of a hundred will just not do what you say. It's not a great feeling when some idiot motorist doesn't see you until the last second, slams on the brakes, and skids right up to your kneecaps! I've had that happen a couple of times.

10-8

I hate it when some honcho or city bigwig lives or moves onto one of our small side streets that has a stoplight. Invariably he or she will complain about the long red light for one little side street, and all of us on the main drag will now have to be held up by some stupid red light that lasts forever.

10-8

One time this gal stole a boombox from our local Kmart. Only one problem: She'd just used her driver's license and military ID photograph to get a check cashed, so we had her picture and her address. This pudgy security guy from the store and I go up to the PD in the town where this gal lives, call her up, and tell her to come in to the PD. But she doesn't. So my backup and I decide to go to her house, which is in a real bad neighborhood. Which is why we didn't want to go there in the first place. Well, this gal is outside her house and we try to arrest her, but a small crowd has materialized out of nowhere and people are shouting about civil rights and riots, and me and my Kmart guy are getting real nervous. Then one local cop shows up, and the crowd disappears like smoke. The coppers must have a pretty bad rep in that neighborhood.

10-8

The first night of midnights is not so bad because you're kind of excited about the novelty of it. But on the second night, the novelty has long since worn off and it's zombie-time out there.

10-8

I'll have to admit that I've been pretty derogatory up to this point, reference my repeated use of the word *scumbag*. I know it makes me sound hard-assed or ignorant. But I can live with that because I believe the word is an apt and very descriptive term that fits well with my line of work. So I use the word a lot, and I will continue to use it. But I feel compelled to give the reader a more specific definition of the word. Here goes. A scumbag is far better described by what he or she does than in any other way. A scumbag drives drunk, drives without a license, drives recklessly all the time with little regard for the safety of others, beats up on his or her spouse, abuses people, uses people, abuses alcohol and drugs, sells drugs, assaults people, steals, scams people, rips off, murders, rapes, bullies, extorts, has loud stinky pets, is loud and stinky, plays music too loud, has no manners, is a pig in general, lies or hides the truth, stomps all over other people's rights without cause, pollutes the earth, destroys nature, and is bigoted. It's possible to be a pretty good person in most areas and maybe a scumbag in one or two. There have been some really "nice" serial killers. And it's possible to be a temporary scumbag or a permanent scumbag. It's a matter of choice, as far as I'm concerned. I've been a scumbag on occasion.

10-8

Our uniforms are made mostly out of polyester. I hate polyester!

10-8

A bad thing: another auto accident caused by other drivers gaping at the accident you're already handling. Headache.

10-8

We had this cop who always wore a toupee. Once out on the highway, he got knocked over a wire fence and landed on his back. And I mean knocked out, too. When the paramedics arrived on the scene, he was still lying flat on his back, with his toupee flopped back by his head. They thought he'd been scalped!

10-8

Once I was laying flares down in a pattern at a highway accident scene. When I finished, I looked up to admire my handiwork. Only then did I realize that I had created a perfect funnel, right towards my self and there was a car in that funnel coming right at me! Stupid.

10-8

More than 100 law enforcement officers are killed in the line of duty annually in this country. Every once in awhile our department will receive a teletype over the wire giving a brief description of what happened in some of these killings. This is so we can read and learn how to avoid getting into such situations. It seems like the leading cause of these deaths is complacency on the part of the cop who got killed. It just goes to show that you never know who you're dealing with and you have to stay frosty, all the time.

10-8

One time I saved the lives of two guys and got no recognition for it. I was taking a shortcut through another town late at night when I saw, out of the corner of my eye, what looked like a motorist dispute, with some fisticuff potential, in this apartment complex parking lot. I pulled in, and these two drunk white guys pointed to this black guy and said, "That dude just pointed a gun at us and said he was going to shoot us!" I could tell they both were really drunk because if they weren't they would have gotten the hell out of there. I turned around and talked to the black guy, who said he'd had a driving confrontation with the two idiots out on the street. He followed the two guys into the parking lot to teach them a lesson. I asked the black guy if he had a gun. It turns out that he was a security guard and did have a gun on him. I didn't even ask to see it. I told the two drunks to get the hell out of there, and I cut the other guy loose. God knows what would have happened if I hadn't been driving by.

10-8

Once the shift commander and I were dispatched on a well-being check. Things were not looking good. In the first place, the call was at an apartment complex where old people lived. The lady we were supposed to check on hadn't been seen for two days. Two or three untouched dinners were stacked outside the door of her apartment. We had the building manager unlock the door. Just inside was the living room and a ghastly sight. The bloated, naked body of a woman the color of alabaster was lying on the living room floor. She appeared to have been dead for at least two days. That is, until she moved and both me and the lieutenant almost fell down. Another misdiagnosis, but it never fails to startle me.

10-8

Alzheimer's disease is pretty tragic. We've got a few older women in town who have it. They're lonely. Sometimes they call the PD. When we get there they do stuff like point to the empty living room and say there are intruders in there. Or they peer real closely at the fabric pattern on the sofa and say there are people in there. Most of the time, we find them wandering around town, totally lost. We take them home and try to contact a relative in those situations. It's sad because we can tell they have intelligent minds, but the disease won't let them put their thoughts together.

10-8

Once this drunk was trying to get his huge, old Dodge pickup started at night in our Kmart parking lot. He was underneath it fiddling with the starter when lo and behold, the thing fires up. It's in gear, it takes off, rolls over his chest. He grabs the front stabilizer bar in a panic, and the truck drags him about 100 feet. It would have made it out onto the highway and rolled all the way to Milwaukee if it hadn't smashed into the Salvation Army trailer parked near the exit. The guy walked by himself over to Dunkin' Donuts and called his sister. But he was really hurting when I saw him in the hospital emergency room.

10-8

Once I was helping these two guys who were attempting to start a small Bobcat bulldozer. I was blocking traffic on this side street with my squad while one guy in a dump truck was towing the other guy in the Bobcat backwards, to get it started. Well, it worked, but the guy in the Bobcat didn't know how to run it. Some of the controls must have been in the "On" position when the thing started, because the front bucket on the Bobcat was going up and down, up and down, smashing the hood of the dump truck. The guy in the dump truck was yelling at the guy in the Bobcat. The guy in the Bobcat was scared to death because he couldn't control the thing. It was funnier than hell to watch these two guys screaming at each other while the Bobcat kept pounding the heck out of the dump truck. Finally, the guy in the dump truck got out and turned the Bobcat off.

10-8

We had this one cop who partied too much and could not stay awake on day shift, especially on weekends. So he devised a little plan. He would go to this entrance ramp on the highway and sit there pretending to run radar. He would prop himself up so the gun could be seen, but he would keep his head back behind the door post of the squad and snooze. Sometimes for hours. Passing motorists always caught on somehow. You could tell he was snoozing because traffic would whiz by at about 80, and he would never pull out.

10-8

Many times people come into the PD to report a hit-and-run accident involving their cars, when really they just hit some fixed object. I had this one guy who tried to say that another car had struck his while it was parked in a parking lot. Only there were pieces of concrete and safety-yellow traffic paint on his rear bumper. I gave him a vague insurance note. Another time this young gal with a bad driving record tried to tell me, in front of her mother, that the family car had been hit while it was parked on the street in front of a friend's house. Except that the bands of white paint and orange paint matched up quite well with our city construction barricades! Hit-and-run accident? Not!

10-8

Once I arrested this guy on the highway for DUI. He didn't have his driver's license on him but gave me a name and date of birth that came back on a valid license. The weight was way off, which made me kind of suspicious. When we got to the PD, he refused a breath test, which made me even more suspicious. But I wrote him four tickets under the name he'd given me. While doing the arrest sheet, he made the mistake of giving me his real home phone number, which I traced to a completely different name. I looked that name up in our local computer and found out we had arrested this guy for a revoked driver's license the previous year. I locked the guy up and rewrote all the tickets under the right name. When his cash bond arrived I handed him his tickets under the right name. He was mad as hell. Too bad.

10-8

Me and this other copper went on a goofy well-being check at this house not far from the PD. It was goofy because a guy called and told us that he had tried calling home and no one answered, and he said that was suspicious. But it was 9:00 in the morning, his wife worked a day job and his two kids were at school, so nobody should have been home anyway. We went over to his house and saw a slit screen on a first-floor bedroom window. The other copper looked at me, I looked at him, we said the hell with it and entered the house through that window, which was not locked. Inside, the bedroom was really spooky, loaded with all kinds of occult stuff. We could tell the guy's teenage daughter lived in there. There was a small electric fan still running on the dresser, and we called out, but got no response. Then we saw a weird glow coming from underneath what we thought was the bathroom door. We were feeling just a little edgy by then, and neither one of us wanted to open the door, fearing what might be on the other side. Finally, I opened the door. It turned out to be a closet. There was a grow-lamp and some marijuana plants in there. I went and got a search warrant and we charged the gal with possession. After the whole thing went down, we figured out that the father knew about the marijuana but wouldn't confront his daughter over it, so he got us to do it for him.

10-8

We had this young homeless guy named Joe in our town. He was a high school track and football star who got strung out on drugs. His parents lived in town, and we were always arresting him for breaking into their basement to get out of the weather. He was a pretty nice guy; clean, too. Once I brought him to the PD on Christmas and gave him some sandwiches. Well, he managed to get himself down to Florida, and we hadn't seen him for awhile. But apparently the PD in the town where he was living down there passed the hat and got him bus fare back to our town. Thank you very much. The last I heard of Joe, some rich lady had taken him under her wing and he was doing pretty good.

10-8

I've seen cars involved in fatal accidents that you could still get in and drive away from the scene. I've seen cars that were just blasted into a million pieces, and the drivers were walking around at the accident scene. It's strange how either your number's up, or it isn't.

10-8

Hospitals can perform miracles. Once there was this poor guy working on his car when the fan blade broke while the engine was still running and a shard of it slashed three-quarters of the way through his neck. The guy was rushed to our hospital, and he not only lived, he completely recovered!

10-8

Being a cop means you have to go into some strange houses! The worst are the P.O.S.E. (Piles of Shit Everywhere) houses. We have one house in town that is so crammed with worthless stuff that you can't even get in the front door. Which is okay with me, because I don't want to go in there, anyway.

10-8

If I should die in the line of duty, I would prefer it to be for a worthy cause, like saving the life of another person. I don't want to get aced by some scumbag who got the drop on me because I was lax for one moment.

10-8

Things that I hope and pray for: peace on earth, good will between men; man making the earth a better place, instead of destroying it and ultimately himself. I wish for harmony, harmony that willingly comes through focusing on certain worldwide goals. I wish for mankind to use clear thinking to address the problems of pollution, wars, famine, drugs, racism, and poverty. I hope that we find solutions to these problems, solutions that seem to have evaded us so far. I pray that our spiritual level will reach and surpass the level of our technology. Technology can only go so far without understanding, cooperation, and long-range planning.

10-8

One night while I was running a little stationary radar patrol at this one location, a woman who lived across the street came out and brought me a cup of coffee. She owed me nothing, and gave without asking me for anything. That is the *only* time that has ever happened to me on this job. I will never forget her small act of kindness.

10-8

Some things that I fear as a cop: hitting a child with my squad car on the way to a call; riots; stone killers; gangs; having to use my gun; child abusers; crazed drug addicts; drug dealers; drunk drivers; getting fired or sued or suspended without pay; losing control of a situation; losing control of myself; harming or killing innocent people; getting hurt or killed on the job.

10-8

We have a local community center for our kids. It's well-located, well-equipped, and well-funded. I'm all for offering our youth alternative forms of recreation, but I do worry that the kids we, as cops, need to focus on, the troublemakers, won't go to the center because to do so would be considered uncool. I believe that promoting our community centers to these kids is a major key in getting them off the streets and into a safe but enjoyable environment.

10-8

A big thank you to those people who aren't afraid to stop and lend a hand at the scene of serious motor vehicle accidents. I can't help but get a good feeling when I see a stranger hold and comfort somebody who's injured.

10-8

I'm not real big on car phones. I'm bigger on concentrating on what's ahead on the roadway. I've handled more than one car accident where one of the drivers was on the phone when the accident happened.

10-8

A really scary future: people in our society so stressed out from the pressure that the government has to mandate drug use. Or people living almost completely vicariously in an attempt to escape the "dullness" of reality. Or the will of human beings given up to computers.

10-8

Once we had a car thief who just took cars that were left running in the parking lots of convenience stores. How convenient! He got away with eleven until he ran into me, or my roadblock, I should say. One day our man grabbed a car at about 11:00 in the morning, a Yellow Cab for God's sake. This happened in a town kind of far away, and although I was working, I wasn't too excited about it. Well, at about 1:00 in the afternoon I'm driving around, minding my own business, when I hear three words screamed out on our areawide band. "Eastbound on 22!" We have a Route 22 in our town, and it sounded kind of close, so I started up that way. Pretty soon it was evident that some state troopers had spotted this stolen cab and are chasing it right into our town limits. So I blasted up to this T-intersection and started making my own little roadblock. There I was stopping traffic, telling this guy in the Jaguar to pull over here, and that guy in the BMW to park it over there. In very short order I had a wall of $30,000 to $50,000 cars completely blocking the road. At the last second the perp, with two state squads in hot pursuit, crested the rise, saw the roadblock, yanked the wheel, and did the most perfect left-hand turn at 60 mph I've ever seen, onto what I know is a very short, dead-end street. Our guys were right with him. So I said, "Yeah!" and jumped in my squad car and went screeching over there, only to be greeted by a very pleasant sight: two big-old-boy troopers whaling on this long-haired punk they've got on the ground next to the stolen cab. I ran up and said, "All right, you got him!" At which point one of the troopers looked up and said, "This is the *passenger*. The driver ran that way." That way was a path that lead into a woods. So I did the stupid thing and ran right in there. I got all of three steps before I was knee-deep in mud. Great, just great. We surrounded the perimeter of the woods, and then called for the dog and the helicopter. They both got there at about the same time, and it took them about seven minutes to flush out the scumbag. We got our man. I laughed when I saw the guy. He was a skinny, eighteen-year-old kid, with only one arm! What a driver! A perfect 90° turn with only one arm! It took me over an hour to clean the mud off my shoes. I had to change my pants. It took me a little longer to realize how stupid it was to make a roadblock out of other people's cars.

10-8

A strange thing I found on the highway: the front end of a green, 1984 T-Bird. I made a sculpture out of it.

10-8

Sometimes we get a serious case where it's dark and the suspect has just fled the scene on foot. That's when we call out K-9. In the old days, we had to wait for another department's dog; now we have one of our own. Whenever the dog shows up on the scene, we're told to get inside our cars, for two reasons. One is so we don't confuse the scent trail for the dog. The other reason is to keep the hell out of the way so the K-9 doesn't get too excited and take a chomp out of us! Hey, it's happened.

10-8

Let me explain in further detail the real monster part of the cop job: shift change. I hate shift change. So do a lot of cops and their families. Shift change, as near as I can figure it, is like having terminal jet lag. We change shifts on the first day of every month, forever. And we rotate backwards. We work a month of days (7:00 AM to 3:00 PM), then change to a month of midnights (11:00 PM to 7:00 AM), and then we swing to the evening shift (3:00 PM to 11:00 AM) for a month. It takes a few weeks to get adjusted to the new shift. So just when your poor body is getting used to one eating-sleeping-shitting cycle, it's time to change the whole game plan. Unless we hook inside jobs at the police department, we'll rotate shifts for our entire twenty years, even if we make sergeant or lieutenant. Not good. Believe me, it gets harder to change shifts the older we get. And don't think our bodies don't let us know what we're doing to them in so many subtle ways. Like a good case of the runs or the clay-in-your-head feeling. There are a few good things about shift change. One is, if I get bored with one shift, I don't have to wait too long for a change. And with these hours, I usually don't get caught in a traffic jam coming from or going to work every day. Big deal. Several studies have shown that rotating shifts takes years off of your life expectancy. I've been doing it for my entire career, and I still feel funny about getting ready to go to work at 10:00 o'clock at night.

10-8

Another great moment in policing: me standing sheepishly by this big pond in the middle of a golf course packed with hackers, with my shotgun out. Assignment: fire off a shotgun round to start a golf tournament! Give me a break. At the time I figured, What the heck, I might as well aim down into the water for safety's sake, right? Wrong! Imagine my dismay as I cut loose and watched my load skip merrily all the way across the pond right toward where some golfers were standing at the other end! I was just waiting for one of them to drop. Thank God no one did! But it looked like a close thing to me.

10-8

So it's suddenly 3:00 in the afternoon and you've just finished working a day shift and you have to come in that night for a midnight shift. Just try going to sleep on a sunny afternoon when you get home. Just try.

10-8

What I fear most about our future: the loss of individuality; the deple-
tion of the earth's resources; the fact that technology is racing so far
ahead of our understanding of its ramifications and our own spiritual
and personal growth; the total or partial breakdown of "normal" society, due to racial prejudice, drug use, crime out of control, mass hys-
teria, et cetera. I also fear that we may be forced to sacrifice personal freedom for "a better tomorrow" or for somebody else's religious
values. Sometimes I wonder if all those things could be due to man's
gradual lessening of contact with the earth and the gradual erosion of
certain basic family values attributable to the gradual erosion of the
basic nuclear family.

10-8

A serious missing link in our local criminal justice system is non-
police people to act as liaisons between the PD and local crime victims, between the PD and local criminals and even potential local
criminals. This kind of work has the possible double impact of easing
the suffering of crime victims and preventing future crimes. How
about criminals themselves assisting crime victims as a part of their
public service? Under strictly supervised conditions, of course. These
ideas are not new, but they could be acted upon just the same. There
are numerous ways to get qualified people to help with this stuff, without having to shell out a huge buck in the process.

10-8

Once while I was moving a car out of the way for the paramedics on
an ambulance call at this house, I did yet another dumb thing. I was
in such a hurry to move this car that I didn't close the driver's door all
the way. So as I was backing up in this narrow driveway, I suddenly
heard this sickening crunch. The driver's door, although only open
about nine inches, managed to get snagged on the side of a little hill
and was peeled all the way forward, kind of like a butterfly wing. It
was pulled so far forward that the outside edge of the door was touching the front bumper. It was very embarrassing for me, to say the
least, to have to explain to this woman what I had just done to her car.

I was able to bend the door back far enough to wire it shut with a coat hanger so she could drive it.

10-8

One time at 5:30 in the morning, I was dispatched to an injury accident on the highway where a car went the wrong way and struck two other cars. When I got there, the first car I saw was a plain blue Dodge (kind of like my squad car) with a drunk guy and a police radio in it. I figured it was just some jamoke from the city who got drunk and then got lost. My supervisor arrived on the scene and gave me the option to punt the accident to another officer because it was near the end of my shift. I was very angry, because in one of the other cars a young woman had suffered an explosive fracture of the right femur, so I said I'd take the paper. In the hospital emergency room, as I was writing up the DUI tickets on the drunk driver, another cop who was assigned to help me came into the ready room and told me that my arrestee was the chief of police in a nearby town. Great. They had put him in a bay next to the young woman with the leg injury. I can remember hearing her screams while I read this guy the DUI warnings. He refused to take any tests. Ultimately, he ended up pleading to the DUI and was forced to resign as chief. I felt bad about the whole thing, until this same guy was involved in another accident involving drinking, where teenagers were hurt.

10-8

Gangs. There's nothing intrinsically wrong with being in a "gang." A gang is just another way for men or women to form small support groups in which to experience friendship and common purpose. In today's society, we are isolated while, at the same time, being buried among billions. Gangs, clubs, fraternities, sororities all serve to give the individual member a kind of instant support group, a sense of identity, and a sense of belonging. Where gangs go *awry* is in their purpose, or what they do. Gangs can accomplish what an individual cannot, be they good things or bad. A gang can clean up a neighborhood, or deal drugs in that neighborhood. A gang can start a carwash or a business or a band or a sports club or a dance club, or it can focus on murder, auto theft, burglary, drug dealing, weapons sales, and vandalism. A gang can seek out kinship or cooperation with other gangs, or it can seek to fight with and to kill members of other gangs. Gangbangers will argue that they joined a gang for protection from other gangs. That doesn't wash with me. If gang members chose to make a contribution instead of doing crimes, what would they need protection for? Very little is done in our major metropolitan areas to encourage gangs to make a *positive* contribution to their communities. Throwing money at gangs, such as what was done in the past, will not work. How about low-interest business loans? Cooperation from local businesses? Sports leagues? Anything to quell the rising tide of self-perpetuating gang violence. Something new is needed to encourage the positive potential for gangs.

10-8

One time the coppers in the local PD just to the south of us were chasing a teenage burglary suspect on foot through a large enclosed park that borders on our town. We were very short-handed on the road that day, and when our dispatcher asked our shift commander, a lieutenant, over the radio if we should send a few bodies over there to help, he calmly replied, "Ah, let them fuck with it." He was so smooth about it that I don't think anybody even heard him say it. We laughed about that one.

10-8

One time a lady in our town contacted us regarding her adult son who was missing from the residence. Our copper rolled over there, took the report, then left. That was late in the evening. The next morning, as the lady was looking out the kitchen window, she saw her son hanging from a tree in the backyard.

10-8

In the town north of us, dog calls are a big deal. When their cops "capture" one, they call in for a rap sheet on the dog.

10-8

Once I got sent to the end of a street in town to look for a tornado!

One of our guys whispered, "Auntie Em, Auntie Em" into the radio. And no, the tornado was not there when I arrived.

10-8

One time by pure chance, I saw lightning strike an electrical power transformer during a storm that caused a major power outage in our business district. Because I saw exactly which transformer was hit, I was able to direct the power company right to the source of the outage, thus saving myself and some of the other cops about an hour of directing traffic in the rain at busy intersections where the traffic lights had gone out. I was real happy about this when I got back in my squad, and I was driving around talking to myself, pumping myself up, calling myself Old Eagle-eye and other crap like that. Well, I didn't know it, but I'd failed to turn my portable radio off when I got back into my squad. Worse yet, it was under my raincoat and somehow the send button was stuck on. So everything I said for a few minutes was broadcast out over the air! The next time I went into the PD to drop off a report, the dispatcher said, "How's it going, Eagle-eye?" Then I knew. But, hey, at least I didn't say anything bad.

10-8

Once I got stuck with this hit-and-run accident right off the bat when I first came on to a day shift on a Sunday morning. This guy who lived on this one corner in our town called up and said, "There's a river running through my front yard!" Not good. So I rolled over there and he was right because some asshole had taken a turn too wide and knocked a fire hydrant clean off at ground level. I took the report and called the public works crew to come fix the hydrant. Later that same day, after being shifted to another beat in another part of town, I was driving by this dead-end street when I spotted this car parked halfway up on the curb two blocks down with a nice, hydrant-sized indentation in the front bumper. Complete with red-and-yellow paint transfer. It turned out that the owner was this gal who got drunk down in the city and plowed into the fire hydrant on the way home. Leaving the car out on the street was not too smart. I got a commendation for solving that caper.

10-8

Once while I was on-duty, I heard a strange call given out to the PD just north of us. "Car so-and-so, respond to such-and-such for a car in a tree." For real. Is that a violation? Can you write somebody a ticket for "car in a tree?"

10-8

For all motor vehicle traffic accident reports, we have to list all the passengers, including their full names, ages, addresses, and phone numbers. I once had the nightmare of all accidents, a loaded school bus versus a van full of Polish maids! The kids on the school bus weren't too hard. I just handed them a clipboard with a blank sheet of paper on it and told them to fill in their information and then pass the clipboard around. However, none of the Polish maids could speak English. Funny how all the maids had the same age, address, and phone number. Quite a coincidence, wouldn't you say?

10-8

We have one good thing going for our department. Two guys from each shift come in an hour early and handle all the paperwork cases that happen during the last hour of the previous shift. This saves cops from catching paper at the end of their shifts, definitely cutting down on overtime. If you're on my department and you make it to the last hour of your shift, chances are real good that an Hour Man will catch any paper that comes along, allowing you to make a timely exit when the whistle blows.

10-8

Fireworks are illegal in our town. One Fourth of July me and this other cop confiscated hundreds of dollars worth of fireworks from the local populace during the daylight hours. After dark we went behind this school and set them all off ourselves. Well, some jerk called in a fireworks noise complaint about the fireworks we were setting off, and we both got dispatched to the call. But we were already there causing the complaint, so we waited a minute or two and then called out that we were on the scene but were unable to locate any problem in the area. And you could hear the fireworks we were setting off booming in the background while we were saying this on the radio.

10-8

I love dogs. But I hate to handle dog calls when I'm supposed to be a cop. Now, I know I can punt a dog call if the dog is running around loose. I just say over the radio that I can't catch it or I can't see it. But if somebody is holding a stray dog, there's nothing I can do but go over there, pick up Fido, and take him to the dog pound. I hate that. I once tried letting a dog jump out of my squad and run away, but the dumb sucker got picked up by somebody else right at the end of my shift so I got stuck working overtime with that mutt.

10-8

How to minimize your loss in a burglary: keep most of the good family jewels in a safety deposit box at the bank. Or hide the stuff in a very unusual place. Professional burglars are looking for jewels, cash, and other small valuables. The less of that stuff you have lying around at home, the less of it you're going to lose. And moms, if you really want to see the family heirloom jewelry sprout legs and walk, just let your daughters take that stuff to college. You might as well just give it away, because for sure it's gonna end up stolen.

10-8

One time when I was standing in the hall waiting for the elevator in our court building, a friend of mine who is a good defense attorney turned around and said, "You know, today I am going to argue a motion on a case that I know I'm going to lose. I hate that." I said, "But it's your job." He went ahead and did it, because he is a good defense attorney.

10-8

Once I went on this suicide call in our town. A middle-aged man who had gone through a divorce and some business setbacks gassed himself in his car inside this garage. It was strange, looking at a human being whose body was frozen in time. It was weird because so much of him was left behind. He left numerous letters to his family and friends in envelopes in the car with him.

10-8

The driving record for motorcyclists in our town is nothing short of outstanding. I've handled very few accidents involving motorcycles despite a lot of bikers rolling on our streets. I'm sure I've only written tickets on two or three in my entire career. I figure that they have fewer accidents and drive better than other motorists because they know their bodies and faces are hanging out there all the time, so they pay attention. On Sundays when the weather is good, tons of bikers converge on this little restaurant in our town to drink coffee and walk around and talk bikes. There are many hardcore bikers in that group, and yet we never, ever have a problem or a complaint there. We don't bother them, and these people motor in, have a good time, and motor out with no hassles. Twice the motorcycle dealership in our town sponsored an all-night party with thousands and thousands of bikers. Both times there were no accidents and no complaints. Biking isn't my thing right now, but I have a lot of respect for the bikers who have come my way.

10-8

There are a lot of speedy motorcycles out there on the streets these days. Big, powerful, sleek crotch-rockets that top out at speeds over 150 mph. Would I get in a pursuit with one of those babies? Not!

10-8

There is this one guy I've arrested a few times who I will never forget. I first met Tim one afternoon when he caused a rear-end motor vehicle accident in our town while driving drunk and with a revoked license. I was impressed by him from the very beginning because he was honest with me. He didn't try to lie to me about who he was or that his license was revoked or that he was drunk. He was also straight-up about being gay, about being an alcoholic, and about being hooked on drugs. When I went to process Tim he even told me that he had AIDS. I really appreciated that. Tim is a good mechanic when he can stay off the booze and the drugs. At one time, when he was very young, he even had his own business and was making good money. Then one night he experimented with drugs at a party. His life has been a downhill slide ever since. He was diagnosed with AIDS a few years ago. He talked to me freely about the night sweats, the strange sores, and being tired all the time. But Tim is a survivor. He doesn't give up. He still works part-time as a mechanic for a land-scaping company in our town. He rarely complains, and he tries not to dwell too much on his situation. Even though I've arrested him he doesn't hold it against me. He still has a sense of humor. From time to time, he hits the bottle pretty heavy. When he does he attracts cops like a magnet. I once asked him what was the most alcohol he ever drank at one sitting, and he told me that once he drank thirty-eight shots of tequila on a bar bet. He got two dollars for every shot he drank after his opponent dropped out at twenty-five. So for twenty-six dollars he almost poisoned himself to death. The last time I saw Tim was at the hospital. Although he appeared to be okay and was taking AZT, he had noticeably lost weight. He was in the emergency room that time for back problems. I like Tim because he's honest and spunky. I wish him the best, wherever he is.

10-8

We spend about a bazillion hours driving around in our squad cars, so the odds alone dictate that sooner or later we are going to come into unintentional contact with one fixed object or another. It could be a rock, a ditch, a pole, part of a building, whatever. But it will happen, and when it does do we call the supervisor over, have an accident report made, and then get gigged for it? Or do we get out a hammer and some handy-dandy white-out and do a little roadside body work? I myself prefer white exterior enamel for the larger stuff.

10-8

Once we had this popular guy on our department make sergeant. Which was good, because we all like the guy. But one day soon after he made rank, there was a complaint on his shift about two cops meeting in a park for two hours on a Sunday morning. This particular beef came from the chief, so the sergeant thought he could make some points by finding out who the culprits were. He felt he could rely on his good personal relationships with the patrolmen to solve the big caper. There were eight guys on the shift that day, and he talked to each guy. And got eight nos. Only then did he discover that no matter how popular he was before, when he made sergeant he crossed that invisible line that always separates regular cops from supervisors. He went from being a friend to being "the enemy."

10-8

We have this one-block area in our downtown business district where the wanna-be-bad kids hang out on weekend nights. Which is okay with me because I certainly prefer being able to see where these people are. I worry a lot more when I can't see them.

10-8

I'm a cop. I don't do and never will do what drunk-driver defense attorneys say I should or shouldn't do. If I acted strictly according to their goofy rules, no one would ever get stopped, and if they did, they'd never be arrested. And if they were, they would never be found guilty, and then maybe 100,000 people would die every year on our highways as the result of drunk driving instead of "only" 18,000.

10-8

The dispatcher job is not an easy one. Out of all of our dispatchers, only one was on before I came on the job. As a dispatcher, you have to deal with a surly public, surly police officers, and unforgiving supervisors. To top it off, if you make a mistake dispatching a call it could cost someone his or her life, so there's a liability factor that comes with the job. One of our new dispatchers worked for us for a few months, but upon finding out about the liability thing, he jumped ship. It takes a person with a certain kind of organization and memory to do the job right. You have to keep track of where all your squads are and what they're doing, answer the phone, talk to people in the lobby, and dispatch and enter calls, sometimes all at the same time.

10-8

What makes a good supervisor? It's hard to say. Ah, maybe it's not so hard. Sometimes it's the intangible things. Other times it's noticeable things, like a good attitude or a stable personality, somebody you can trust to cover you and trust to make good decisions when the shit hits the fan. Somebody who can schmooz just a little. Somebody who knows people and knows their way around town. Somebody who can go and get the right answers. Somebody who's confident enough in our abilities so that he's not over-supervising and looking over our shoulders all the time. Somebody who's fair. Some supervisors I wouldn't give the time of day to. Some supervisors I would die for.

10-8

What makes a bad supervisor? Someone you can't trust. Somebody who is inconsistent. Someone who over-supervises because he or she has no confidence. Somebody who responds to every call, sticks his nose in and screws it up. Somebody who constantly gigs other cops for bullshit and then covers his own ass when he makes exactly the same mistake. Somebody who is automatically inclined to believe some penny-ante jerk's story over what his own cop has to say. Somebody who thinks he's going to get ahead faster by gigging more cops (which doesn't seem to work by the way, thank God).

10-8

One thing that really pisses me off is looking for a drunk driver over an entire midnight shift, not getting one, and then getting stuck behind one on the way home from work!

10-8

The cost of a traffic ticket without court costs went up from $50 to $75 this year. Tickets were only $35 when I became a cop in 1982. Seventy-five seems a little steep to me. Are we trying to keep up with inflation, or what?

10-8

There was this guy who lived in the town where we had to go to court all the time. He used to leave very inflammatory anti-Semitic literature (which he wrote and published himself) under the windshield wipers of our squads. After awhile he seemed to back off a little, but then last year some of the same materials turned up in mailboxes of people who lived right next to our police station. These people weren't even Jewish, but the stuff was so outrageous even they called us to complain. Unfortunately, there really is not much we can do about it.

10-8

I like to have the driver's window down when I'm running stationary radar patrol. It allows me to hear approaching traffic noise, which is an important cue for me in prejudging motor vehicle speed.

10-8

Two things cops should probably not do is own a bar or publicly endorse political candidates.

10-8

The sheriff system of law enforcement works extremely well in many areas of our country. The only beef I have is that a cop who is elected is much more susceptible to political pressure, which in most cases has very little to do with the cop job.

10-8

"Motion to suppress the evidence, motion to suppress the stop, motion to suppress the confession." I get really irate the moment I hear that crap come out of a defense attorney's mouth. What all the legal gob-bledygook means is this: the evidence against the offender is totally damaging, the stop is totally righteous, and the confession is probably the truth. But the defense attorney can't have any of that stuff come out in court. It wouldn't be "fair". Oh no, he has to suppress it, hide it, sweep it under the rug so no one will see it and be able to reach a rightful decision. It's just another ploy that came from God-knows-where so guilty clients can walk. Why don't we suppress crime and criminals instead, by allowing all the truth into a trial, so the crimi-nals can be locked up where they belong?

10-8

As you may be able to tell by now, I have a real problem with too much control. Sure, we're cops and what we do is important, but there is such a thing as too much control on this job. We had this jerk chief who was so anal he was totally into the control thing. He honestly believed that all of his cops were out to screw the department as soon as their squads rolled off the parking lot of the Public Safety Center. He spent big bucks to have vehicle locators installed in all the squads. This was tremendous for morale. The locators turned out to be totally unnecessary, totally a hassle; they didn't work half the time, actually interfered with our police radio transmissions, and were just, in general, a giant pain in the ass. So we don't have them anymore. But more control is looming on the horizon. Up to now, we've been able to fill out our own time sheets, using units of fifteen-minute intervals for each duty day. But supposedly we are getting a new system that will eliminate time sheets. In order for it to work, we will have to report every little thing we do over the air. And artistic license (which I will admit I've used on some of my time sheets) will be eliminated. I've glanced at some of the new paperwork that will be generated by this new system, and it looks like yet another extra pile of crap that I really don't need. Hell, one of the best parts of this job is that once you roll off the lot of the PD at the beginning of the shift, you can do whatever you want, within certain limits.

10-8

There is one bad thing about cops and their testimony in court: We never get to fully explain what went down. We're very restricted in the courtroom. We're rarely allowed to express an opinion of any kind, unless we qualify as an expert witness. Usually we are restricted to only yes-or-no answers. Sometimes crucial testimony or the subtleties of a case aren't fully elicited. Cops should be allowed to explain fully what they did and why they did it. You know the defendant is going to lie to save his own skin. And the cops were there, not the attorneys. So who has the most reliable information?

10-8

I once had a judge believe totally some pay-me-and-I'll-say-anything-you-want-me-to-say, so-called expert witness for the defense. This guy was some old geezer who not only didn't know what he was talking about but actually fell asleep during the proceedings! This man had absolutely no basis for refuting our evidence. He just said it was wrong. The judge took his word as gospel and I lost the case. I will say, though, that this judge has been more than fair to me ever since.

10-8

Maybe I'm lazy, but I just think it's easier for everyone concerned if steps can be taken in certain situations to avoid the entire arrest-charge-court-fines-attorneys-judges scene. Like when a cop calls you at home and says you took something or did something and it's beyond a doubt that you did whatever it was, don't be a jerk. Offer to give it back or go into the PD to work out the problem. Maybe it was only a mistake or a misunderstanding. If you write a bad check and a cop calls you, pay the damn thing, don't delay and hem and haw. It could keep you from being arrested. We had one cop who didn't even bother to call the people on his bad check cases to see if they'd pay up. He just went and got warrants right away. There were quite a few well-to-do women around town who were very surprised when he showed up on their doorsteps and then hauled them down to the PD. Or let's say you're hassling somebody, in person or on the telephone or whatever. If a cop calls you up and tells you to knock it off, do it, okay? Don't be pig-headed and make us have to arrest you. If you get in a fight with your buddy and somebody gets popped but it's not serious and we call you, don't just blow it off. Try to work it out. I'm not going to say that total cooperation with the cops will get you off completely on some things or that it will get you a smaller fine or a lighter sentence, but it could.

10-8

You screw up, you do some big crime and get caught, this is what we should do for you: get DNA samples, semen samples, fingerprints, palmprints, foot- and toeprints, blood samples, a retinal scan, a voiceprint, hair samples, and to top that off, your MO. Then we should put all this stuff in a nice, big computer. When you get released from prison, which you most certainly will these days, we would then put your release information and where you like to hang out in there, too. Then we'd wait for you to do your little thing again, which is another sure thing. And when some cop takes a report on your caper, puts that in the computer, and that sucker spits out your name, then we come pay you a visit. And you won't be able to say, "Hey, it wasn't me, man. My cousin Darryl did it." Yeah, right, your cousin Darryl with the same MO, fingerprints, and DNA?!

10-8

Suck-ups. Yes, we've got 'em in our department. We've got guys who will do anything to get promoted. Like doing personal favors, on their own time, for the top brass. How about even changing religions? True story. We've got guys who join all these special teams just to make some kind of impression. It's sick to see, but this stuff goes on in just about every department. This one cop we had wrote a suck-up letter to get into the detective bureau. It was so outrageous that I keep a copy of it with me and whip it out every once in a while for a laugh. The guy is a sergeant now. We've got other guys stumbling all over each other, racing down the hall to rat out other cops. Not good.

10-8

Our police department is not that big. We work in a nice area. So why do we have a fully equipped, fifteen-man SWAT team that sucks up thousands of dollars in overtime and equipment, when it's never even been called out in four years? I don't know, but don't get on my case about my overtime when I have to finish arrest reports at the end of my shift or when I have to go to court. I don't want to hear about it.

10-8

Discounts and freebies for cops. Yeah, I know, a lot of people piss and moan about cops getting all kinds of deals and free stuff. And I know that, professionally speaking, cops should never accept gratuities. But, hey, it's a tough, thankless job, and we're underpaid for what we have to put up with. We'll never be rich. I think free is a little too much, though. And I don't *demand* a discount; I don't ask for it or even expect it all the time.

We have this old folks home near our south limits. Security there is not so good. In fact, it doesn't even exist. Sometimes we get reports of geezers whizzing down the road to go see their relatives who never visit. Which wouldn't be so bad if they didn't do it in their wheel-chairs!

You guys or gals who like to get your jollies by making harassing or obscene phone calls, I'd personally like to reach right through the telephone lines and strangle the shit out of you. I'm tired of going on phone-call cases and actually picking up the phone of a fifty-nine-year-old woman and hearing some scumbag who wants to eat my panties or some drunk who wants to kick my ass. I've heard lots of really strange stuff on answering machines, too. Folks, these calls are disruptive to *normal* people who are just trying to mind their own business, okay? Real soon, improved software and new hardware is going to catch up with you jerks, anyway. I expect Caller ID and other new telephone services will discourage a lot of you perps, or catch you, which is even better!

Organized crime. It's powerful, it's pervasive, it's gone legit in many ways, it's here to stay, and it scares the hell out of me sometimes. I don't have much of a quarrel with any organization that provides goods and services that people want but that the government is too stupid to get into. That stuff doesn't bother me as much as the out-right assassination of human beings. No matter how low the victim is, murder is still pretty hard to ignore. I just hope that some of the profits from organized crime do get funneled back into the economy some-how. I also hope that mobsters all go or have gone or are taking steps to go legit. Maybe I'm dreaming, but I know one thing: I don't want to be near organized crime or around it myself. I've got too many responsibilities.

10-8

I've trashed defense attorneys pretty well up to now, don't you think? It's time for me to begrudgingly give them some praise. Being a defense attorney takes a special kind of guts, because you're destined to be unpopular if you're good. Cops won't like you, prosecutors will be sick of looking at your face, judges will not like you, bailiffs and other court personnel won't like you (unless they want overtime), your clients won't like you (because they have to keep paying you), and crime victims and society in general won't like you because your job is to get some guilty perp off the hook. It takes a resiliency and *chutzpah* to battle over a case you know you're going to lose. Then you have to deal with the guilt when you actually win a case, get some dirtbag off, and then watch in horror as the perp goes out and kills somebody or something. I suppose there are actual cases out there where the defendant is really not guilty, or the poor sucker deserves a lighter sentence, or he gets an unfair trial the first time around. But those seem to be few and far between. Still, it's in those cases that the defense attorney is absolutely vital to the system. Even guilty people need someone on their side. For the whole system to work, good defense attorneys are essential. They keep the system honest, they keep cops on their toes. I can't help but have a certain respect for the defense attorney who finds an issue or issues in a tough case and really focuses on them and tries like hell to make it work in court. Most of the defense attorneys I know are pretty good people all around. And they really have no one to impress but their clients, the judge, and a jury.

10-8

Okay, so you're like nine-tenths of the normal people on earth and you suddenly find yourself driving around somewhere and you know for sure that you're hammered, plastered, pie-eyed, stinky-drunk, or whatever. Your ears are buzzing like there's a hornet's nest in there, your face and lips are numb, you can't keep your eyes open, you can't see even if you could because there are at least twelve of everything, everything is spinning around, and you can't even feel if your arms and legs are still attached. *Don't keep driving!* Get rid of that car right now. Pull into a driveway, any driveway. Pull off the road, or put it in a parking lot and abandon that sucker, get your body away from it as fast as you can, and search for a phone. Phones are everywhere! Call a cab or a limo or a friend. Call a relative. They'll love you for it because then you'll owe them one. Think through all that alcoholic fuzz. You could be saving your own life, your license, your car, or your job. One phone call to keep all that. We all know that there are going to be times when just about everybody wants and needs to party. I'm not encouraging wanton consumption of alcohol here, I'm just being realistic. If you really feel the need, do it at home. Or use the designated driver. I'm a big fan of that option. Then you can let go a little yourself, without having to worry about driving. Just make damn sure your designated driver doesn't drink too much. I've arrested lots of so-called designated drivers who turned out to be *drinkers* instead.

10-8

Store owners, don't just leave your cash in the register drawer. And don't ever leave big dough in the store overnight, even in a safe. This is stupid. Get that cash in the bank, where it belongs, as soon as possible. And when you take your daily deposit to the bank, please vary your routes and times and cars and bags and carriers so your routine doesn't get pegged and you don't get robbed. Late at night after closing is not a good time to be carrying that bank bag, okay? Using a little smarts could save you a lot of money. It also could save your life or the life of one of your employees.

10-8

Some cops just can't get along with other cops. It's just a personality thing. They just don't belong on the same shift, know what I mean?

10-8

Almost every shift has a heat man: a guy who is always either a screw-up or a real discipline problem or just anti-administration. A cop like this is good to have on your shift because, for one, he makes you look good no matter how bad you are, and two, the supervisors are always on his back, not yours. It's no fun being the heat man. I can tell you from experience.

10-8

Of all the houses I've been in on this job, for whatever reason, I've gotten a definitely spooky feeling in only two. One was murderer Laurie Dann's house. Nothing has been reported yet from the other house. But I'm waiting!

10-8

Have I ever had sex in my squad while in full uniform and on-duty? No comment. Cops are people. We have needs.

10-8

One of our guys got a twenty-nine-day suspension without pay for refusing to leave a traffic post when ordered by a sergeant to come into the station to throw fingerprint dust on a stolen car that was locked up in our garage and wasn't going anywhere. He wouldn't leave his post because he was working at the most dangerous intersection in the whole state, where the traffic lights had gone out with two rookies on; he didn't want to jeopardize their safety by leaving. The sergeant, who was languishing around in the station at the time, was dead wrong for not coming out and assessing the situation. Every other squad was tied up on calls at the time, and he should have gotten his lazy, fat ass out on the road and pitched in. I admire that cop for sticking to his guns. He was right to choose the safety of other officers over a stupid order from a supervisor who had his head up is you-know-what. Of course the administration didn't see it that way. They called it insubordination.

10-8

Every time I bitch about a supervisor, I always run into the same wall, even when the supervisor is obviously wrong. The rule is that we have to do whatever any supervisor says, no matter what. I hate that. I try to see the reasons for it, but I hate it, anyway.

10-8

A well-balanced shift is composed of some new guys who want to go out there and kick some ass, some old guys who know their way around people and the job, and some guys in the middle who are a little bit of both the old and the new.

10-8

The high point of my career: driving around the corner of the water plant one night on a midnight and catching a guy and a gal doing it right in the surf down by the lake. I had my spotlight on them for five minutes before they saw me and stopped what they were doing. I rolled over to the parking lot above them and told them on my PA that I would be back in thirty minutes and could they please be gone by then?

10-8

Some of the pranks I've pulled on other cops I couldn't even tell you about. The statute of limitations isn't up yet!

10-8

One time at the end of a 3-11 shift, I saw another cop gassing up his squad at the pumps behind the PD. I had this huge apple core and just heaved it right over the top of the fire station at that end of the building. It was a totally blind shot and I nailed that poor sucker right on the shoulder! Must have scared the hell out of him, that thing coming out of nowhere. Somehow he figured out right away that I did it.

10-8

This guy on our shift was a real good cop, but sort of chunky. One day when I came to work I noticed he was wearing the exact same blue jeans as me, same brand, same inseam. Only his waist size was a lot larger than mine. His jeans were hanging up in the locker room, so I switched them with mine. I even put his belt in my jeans. Later I saw him picking at some holiday food in the lunchroom, so I gigged him about his weight a little, setting him up for the fall. He even bragged about how well he had done on our last physical-fitness assessment, even though he was "twenty" pounds overweight. I stood by while he tried to shoehorn himself into my jeans a few minutes later. He chased me right out of the PD.

10-8

One time near the end of a long midnight shift, one of my fellow cops threw a tennis ball at me as he drove by. It just so happened that I had picked up a basketball off the road that night, so I turned around right away and threw the basketball at him. That's the only time I was ever one-up on that guy!

10-8

There's nothing so good in life as having a horrible residential burglary go down in your beat while you are busy wolfing down a hamburger and fries at the local fast-food joint. You're busy stuffing your face, and the bad guys are busy stuffing their van chock full of some poor taxpayer's goods. I really get pissed and embarrassed when this happens, but what can I do? A guy's got to eat!

10-8

There's a town north of us that we call The City of No Crime. The people who live there are so rich and so concerned with appearances that they cover up everything, including burglaries, domestic batteries, assaults, and God knows what else, just so their neighbors won't see a squad car in their driveway. I guess having dough is a major incentive to sweep real crimes under the rug.

10-8

I wish everybody knew more about basic crime prevention. So far there doesn't seem to be an easy and interesting way to spread the word around. There should be. Why should people have to wait until they become victims to learn this stuff? By then it's too late.

10-8

Most good cops pay attention to the things they see out of the *corners* of their eyes. That is where a lot of what the bad guys do happens.

10-8

Here's a message to all the women who were abused by their husbands, got up the nerve to do the right thing, got an order of protection, booted the jerk out of the house, but then let the abuser back in the house and then things didn't go right and they got abused again and had to call us over to the house again. *Don't do that!*

10-8

Okay, okay, what about all those cops doing personal business while they're on-duty? As far as I'm concerned, a quick trip or two in and out of a store, a couple of local phone calls, or anything that takes only a few minutes, is no big deal. Cops running a full-time business while on-duty or getting a shampoo, shave, and a haircut are pushing it a little. And by the way, sitting in the donut shop is the same thing as being on-duty to me, okay?

10-8

All cops should have car phones in their squad cars. This is coming. You can say things on the phone that you don't want to give out over the air, in case the bad guys are listening. And believe me, for less than fifteen bucks they can do just that. You can also do follow-up investigations from your squad, instead of having to go to the station or to a pay phone. And by the way, if a cop asks to use your phone, just let him or her do it. If the cop dials Alaska or gets into a prolonged argument with his girlfriend, then you've got the right to complain about it.

10-8

Talk about frustration. How about this? You get a really hot in-progress call, but you just drove by that area where it's going down five minutes ago and now you're too far away to make a pinch. Bummer.

10-8

On the radio, we're supposed to say "affirmative" for "yes" and "negative" for "no." Seven syllables as opposed to only two. Give me a break.

10-8

Drunk driving cuts across *all* social barriers. That is the one place where the rich have to rub elbows with the poor on a regular basis. Whites, blacks, Hispanics, Asians, males, females, rich, poor, young, old, middle-aged, you see them all in DUI court. But out of more than 500 people that I've arrested so far for DUI, fully one-third have been Hispanic. That seems a bit out of proportion, considering local demographics. It indicates to me that there's a real problem there.

10-8

Lawsuits, we've got 'em. We're mired in a very litigious society. My favorite thing is to make an insurance note on some minor fender-bender where there is little or no damage to either vehicle involved and no injuries reported, and then have one party involved come back three days later, after talking to Uncle Lawyer Louie, and try to report a neck or back injury. About a third of our cops get sued at one time or another in their careers. And, of course, I'm lucky enough to be one of them. On the other hand, one of our coppers got some pretty big dough after being flattened by this goofy motorist while directing traffic. So I guess it goes both ways.

10-8

Everybody knows traffic stinks around here. And they know where and when. So why don't they just avoid those bad spots during the peak hours? That sounds pretty good to me. I don't think it's that hard to plan shopping or other errands around the rush hours, do you? Go for that little window between 9:00 and 11:00 in the morning or between 1:30 and 3:30 in the afternoon. Or any night on weekdays after 7:00 would be good. Car pooling, taking alternate routes, or alternate forms of transportation could help here. Or how about just driving less and walking, biking, or skating more? Sometimes I just wish there were no cars, period.

10-8

Why do we wear our badges next to our hearts? Because that is what you need a lot of to do this job.

10-8

It is not that unusual to walk up to someone's door in full uniform, badge shining, portable police radio blaring, fully marked squad behind you in the driveway with lights flashing, and still have whoever answers the door ask you for some ID. Hey folks, anybody can cough up $5 for a fake ID and about $15 for a pretty authentic-looking badge. But the uniform, portable radio, gun, and fully equipped squad are a little harder to get, if you know what I mean. Still, I don't blame people for asking. As a matter of fact, I have to respect someone who is that wary. I suppose there may be a few cop wanna-bes out there who might have all that stuff!

10-8

When you become a cop, you have to learn how to observe in a new way. You have to brush over everything with your eyes and use your training and instincts to alert you to something that is suspicious or out of place. Because there's this huge amount of incoming data, cops can't stay stuck on each insignificant detail. We constantly have to brush and discriminate, brush and discriminate. This becomes a habit that is very hard to break out of when we're not on the job.

10-8

Is the profuse violence portrayed on television and in the movies affecting viewers? I can't really say for sure. But I believe that our brains take in and process everything we see, hear, and feel. So all that violence we are exposed to is in there, somewhere. I don't know what it's doing. Maybe different things to different people. I'm absolutely sure that it doesn't just go away. There's a lot of it out there, and I watch, have watched, and probably will continue to watch this stuff. I wish we had some conclusive evidence, but the human brain and how it functions is still much of a mystery to me. I'm afraid that we will find out too late just how inured we "watchers" have become to violence.

10-8

Ask me, and I'll be the first one to tell you that I'm not the greatest cop who ever walked upon the face of the earth. I'm willful, and I've got a temper that I keep very well under control. I am moody and absolutely surly sometimes; when I am, I show it. I also have this tendency to blow off a lot of minor stuff. I should follow up more on cases. I should concentrate more on public relations, community contacts, and the development of informants. And if you can't tell by now, I chafe under very strict supervision. I may not be ideally suited for the cop job, but that's what I do, so you'll have to take it or leave it; that's just the way I'm made. Uh, did I mention that I might concentrate on traffic arrests a little too much?

10-8

How to avoid being burglarized: Use stout locks on your apartment doors and stout locks or bars on your apartment windows. Avoid living in a house on a dead-end street, or in a house with a woods or a park or a golf course in your backyard. When you go on vacation, cancel your mail and other deliveries, and that includes the newspaper, too. Nothing says *Come burglarize me* like six newspapers piled up in the driveway. Have somebody live in or look after your house while you're gone. Notify the local PD when you leave and when you'll be coming back. Keep cars in your driveway and try to have them moved around. Set lights, TVs and radios on timers to give the outward appearance that someone is home. Get an alarm system, if you feel the need. An alarm company sticker on a front window might make burglars skip your house and move on to another that doesn't have an alarm. Have nosy neighbors. Install exterior lights that turn on automatically when a car or person enters your yard or your property. Be suspicious, not paranoid, about unusual activity or strangers in your neighborhood. Spread out your potential break-in losses by hiding valuables or keeping them in the bank. And that goes for collections, too. Wall safes may be a good idea. Always remember, the best defense against burglars is not to have anything worth taking.

10-8

If you have a complaint about speeding cars on your street, call us and let us set up radar in your driveway so we can catch and cite violators: your neighbors.

10-8

I love it when I'm driving in uniform, in a marked squad, on a clear sunny day doing 65 in a 55 on the highway and some jerk passes me. What is that person thinking, Oh, there's a speeding cop, I'll just pass him up quietly and maybe he won't notice?

10-8

Four things I need to have for proper stationary patrol: a radar unit in good working condition; a well-posted speed limit sign; fairly good weather; and you approaching my position in a speeding vehicle.

10-8

IAD. Three little initials that strike fear into the hearts of cops: Internal Affairs Division. In short, cops whose job it is to investigate other cops. Most smaller departments, like ours, just use the chief or the deputy chief and the poor copper's supervisor to conduct investigations into beefs against cops. The larger PDs can afford the luxury of having one cop or an entire division of cops dedicated solely to Internal Affairs. Hey, on any given day there are hundreds of thousands of cops out on the street making millions of decisions. Somebody is bound to screw up somewhere. I know I have. And I got investigated and suspended. And *some* of the times I even deserved it. It comes with this job. On my department, if you've done something really bad, they might put a detective on your case. Just thinking about that gives me the willies.

10-8

We have some full-time detectives. Almost to a man they are both expert and doggedly determined investigators. That's why they are in the dick bureau. They do all the tedious legwork: follow-ups, phone calls, a lot of warrants, stakeouts, drug busts, and going outside the limits of our jurisdiction on investigations; the real nuts and bolts of police work. They also do background checks on prospective employees for the PD and for liquor-license applicants. Sure, they end up doing a lot of clerical and gofer-type stuff, but all in all, it's a pretty good job. You get to wear real clothes instead of the polyester blue monkey suit. You usually don't have to rotate shifts, except maybe from days to afternoons if you are with our department. And although it's a lateral transfer without any increase in pay over that of a regular patrolman, it's considered a status job. Our detectives have a lot of discretion when it comes to handling their cases. Each detective has at least one specialty. One has a K-9. One or two are arson investigators. One is a hostage negotiator. There are some drawbacks. Detectives are under the nose of the brass a lot. If you're a detective you may have to carry a beeper even off-duty, and be on call, sometimes being paged in the middle of a party or in the dead of night. Your hours may be subject to drastic increases when hot cases occur and time is of the essence. Our detectives have worked major cases for over thirty-six hours at a stretch without a break. They usually catch the big capers like burglaries, robberies, homicides, rapes, suicides, and certainly those politically sensitive cases that pop up every once in awhile and are a huge pain in the ass. A sharp detective bureau is a very positive asset to any police department.

10-8

We have one juvenile officer who handles most of the cases that come through our PD involving persons under age. He is one busy guy, let me tell you.

10-8

When one of our supervisors was chasing this garage burglar around on one of our golf courses, he did a very dumb thing. When he spotted the perp, he was in such a hurry to get out of his squad and get after the dirtbag, that he forgot to put the squad car in PARK. As a matter of fact, he left it running, and in gear, and on an incline leading to a pond. Which wouldn't have been so bad except for the fact that he left one of his cops locked in the back seat at the time! And the cop was too big to squeeze through the partition between the front and back seats! After a brief moment of pure panic, the lieutenant did manage to get back into his squad before it dived into the pond. But he ran off again, still leaving the cop locked in his squad! They did catch the bad guy in the end.

10-8

Once one of our cops was helping this gal fix a flat tire out on the highway. Another car pulled up behind his squad, flashing its bright lights at him. The driver got out of the car, walked up to the copper and pointed back to his car. He said only one word, "Trouble." And there was. There was a forty-four-year-old guy slumped in the front passenger seat. He was still warm, but very dead, too. The poor guy had just had the big one in the car.

10-8

Missing-person cases can be interesting. Or scary. Usually with us, it's just teens who get in an argument with Mom and run away to a friend's house for a day or two. But we had this one guy who was gone for six months! We'd just about given up hope on the kid when somebody found him working on a farm in Pennsylvania or something. We did have a nightmare case, though. A nice local kid went out to dinner with his parents one night. After dinner he told them he was going downtown to party a little. Well, he never came home. His car was found abandoned on a highway spur just south of our town. Turns out that he was most likely picked up by a serial killer, because his remains were eventually found buried in a rural area in the northeastern part of our county. Most everybody does turn up, sooner or later.

10-8

Once one of our cops who is now a deputy chief parked his squad on the shoulder of the highway and walked away from it for a second. When he turned around, it was gone! He had left it in NEUTRAL and it rolled down an embankment and he had to have it towed out of there.

10-8

There's nothing like telling some guy that you think he might be drunk, while he's leaning up against his car and denying it. And his car is out in the middle of this field about 200 feet from the roadway. Come on!

10-8

You want to see a bunch of cops zoom in on an area real fast, give us a missing-child call. We get scared when we get those, because the possibility of a true abduction is always lurking at the back of our minds. An abduction with no leads would be a nightmare for us. We do know that the best place to start looking for a missing child is always in the immediate area, such as in a closet in the house or at a nearby friend's house. We get really nervous if the kid doesn't show up in thirty minutes or so. Usually we broadcast a local lookout giving the kid's description and possible whereabouts. And usually the kid pops up somewhere. Whew!

10-8

Bad cops. Yeah, there are a few. What do bad cops do? Well, some steal stuff. Some solicit and take bribes. Some steal and then deal drugs. Some extort businesses for protection money. Some actually run or work for gambling or prostitution or theft rings. Some just beat the shit out of people with little or no provocation. Some are paranoid. Some are maniacs. Some are mentally very unsound. Some are trigger happy. Some are alcoholics. Some are drug addicts. Some think it's okay to trample all over somebody else's civil rights. Some are pathological liars. Some are rapists. Some are perverts. The list is a long one. But remember, cops are human beings. We have the potential to do wrong just like everybody else.

10-8

We had this gal with the Department of Corrections come out to our town. I happened to know where the guy she was looking for was living, so I took her over there. I remember her pretty well because she was absolutely venomous about this guy, calling him a convict and saying that his apartment wasn't really his because wherever a parolee goes is really just an extension of his jail cell. Maybe she was right, but the guy had a few heavy drug pinches on his record and that was about all. She told us she needed a urine sample from the convict as part of his parole. We stood by as he willingly gave the sample. I think he passed that test, but one time before that he flunked a test and they sent him straight back to the slammer for six months or even longer. Brutal.

10-8

Men commit suicide in different ways than women. Men hang themselves, use guns, or run the car in the garage. Women are more likely to use pills and alcohol, or to slit their wrists.

10-8

Some towns have a reputation for writing a lot of traffic tickets. Ours is not one of them. It's been said that strict traffic enforcement reduces the number of traffic accidents. I'd like to see the accident statistics in those towns with the strict reputations and compare them with ours, to see if this is really true. I do know that we used to have about 900 full-report accidents a year in our town, plus a lot of minor accidents that either weren't reported or that only required insurance notes. That seems like a lot to me. Maybe it isn't. Or maybe we just have a lot of bad drivers.

10-8

Cops really fear being sent over to a house on a well-being check and discovering that the husband of the household has killed his entire family, then himself. Without any warning. Without any prior contacts at that house. And without any known reason. You can't recuperate from the horror of that.

10-8

We have a very enterprising young man working our area. He simply intercepts people's personal bank-check pads in the mail. He probably takes them right out of people's mailboxes. He then writes checks to "cash" and rifles the accounts. So far he's netted about $500,000. He's a white male in his early twenties, medium build, brown hair, and glasses. How do I know what he looks like? Banks have pictures of the guy!

10-8

Some people have a lead foot when they drive. Maybe they can't help it. Which is okay with me. Because sooner or later, if you play, you have to pay.

10-8

We have a support-group organization in our town for recurring drug and alcohol abusers. Its members meet weekly in a couple of rooms above some of our shops in the business district. They gather to share their experiences with drug and alcohol abuse, to get a little counseling, and to party every once in a while. I've only been called over there twice, each time for really minor stuff. I never mess with these people. They are living with a monkey on their backs, and they're coming to the club in an effort to try to rebuild their lives. I could run license plates and hassle them, but I just don't want to get in the way of what they need, which is help and support. I respect these people, even though I don't share their experiences. Yet.

10-8

I often wonder how our society measures up against societies from different times and cultures, crime-wise. I'm not sure, but I have a sneaking suspicion that except for a few rare examples, we humans really haven't changed that much. It's hard to tell. Crime data wasn't usually recorded in the good old days. Yes, we all hear about the spiraling crime rates, but given the absolutely huge number of people living so squashed together around here, I'm surprised that more crimes don't occur.

10-8

I have to laugh when I go to DUI court and here's some guy or gal standing up in front of the judge wearing a Jim Beam T-shirt or a Miller baseball cap or something stupid like that. The clothing and the logos are okay with me. But, hey, DUI court is not the place to be flashing that stuff. I've seen some folks who were even dumber. Four times I've seen guys who were quite obviously stinky drunk appearing in front of a judge. Four times the judge told these people to leave the courtroom or be cited for contempt. One judge made a guy go next door to the police station to take a Breathalyzer test! I never heard what the results were or what happened to the guy, but whatever it was, it couldn't have been good.

10-8

Dough. Our town has it. I would definitely consider our little burg to be an affluent suburb. I'm not aware of the exact per-capita income, but I'm very aware of the high cost of real estate and the high taxes paid by the local citizenry. Those high taxes pay our salaries, which are pretty reasonable, I must say. And our people do get top-notch services. We've got thirty-six well tended parks in the city limits, six golf courses, and a lake with swimming and boating beaches. And a fairly low crime rate. All in all, our town is a very nice place to live. Too bad we cops can't afford to live there.

10-8

Prostitution in our town? Yeah, we've got it. Guys driving gals around in the middle of the night. I've stopped a few of these deliverymen, and a few of them are not afraid to tell me exactly what they're doing. And do you know what? Don't expect me to get all hot and bothered about it. I know lonely people need love, physical love. Even people who are not lonely need it. And for one reason or another, some people have to pay for it. Is that a crime? Not in my book. Keep it discreet, low profile, no ripping off, no street flashing, come in, do the job, do it well, and I'm not going to play God and say, "No, you can't do that." On the other hand, I see you walking the streets or some poor dirtbag comes into the PD to report he got ripped off, I may have to do something about it.

10-8

One of our department's policies on stuff like pepper spray is that the officers who are going to be authorized to carry and use certain personal defense items must be exposed to them first before they can unleash them on the general public. Direct translation: I got squirted in the face with this stuff. So now I'm very up-close and personal with the product. What can I tell you? *It works.* It works quickly. And it's pure hell when you're dosed. After ten minutes, I couldn't decide which was worse: the burning sensation on my face, neck and ears that felt like I'd fallen asleep under the sunlamp for eight hours, the stinging in my eyes that felt like somebody threw burning sand in there, or the lava-like heat blasting continuously through my mucous membranes. I felt very near normal after about an hour, though. But now I'd rather strike somebody with a baton and kick them senseless and risk a lawsuit than spray them. As a matter of fact, I'd rather be beaten with a baton and kicked around myself than squirted with that stuff! One officer did say something that was a little prophetic. He said, "With this stuff we'll never have to fight with anybody again." After experiencing what pepper spray can do, he could be right.

10-8

White-collar crime. Rampant increase. Here are a few of the white collar crimes some of our illustrious local citizens have committed: Ponzi schemes of all kinds (the old give me a huge chunk of your hard-earned dough, I'll invest it, you'll get whopping interest...but what I really mean is I'll take all your money, blow it on myself, and then pay you a few bogus premiums or interest payments until I get caught and then I'll either split or declare bankruptcy), bogus real estate deals, medical fraud (a big one), all kinds of illegal stocks, bonds, and options deals, bad business deals. The list goes on. We cops find out about that stuff in some pretty strange ways. Like in the city newspapers. Or when the scammers get their houses burglarized a few times, or they get threatened, or they get beaten up, or warrants for their arrest come down to us from other jurisdictions. We've got some real characters in town, let me tell you. A doctor who allegedly performed *beaucoup* unnecessary surgeries. A con artist who sold a luxury yacht he didn't even own and that wasn't even for sale; he pocketed a cool 80,000 smackers for that one. I dealt personally with this guy all the time on bad check cases, and he always paid up! That particular gentleman went on the lam for quite awhile, until he was caught driving a cab in New York. We've got several lower-level schmucks, both men and women, who just make promises, take people's money, and then don't give it back. White-collar criminals should be locked up with the other animals. I see no difference between one guy robbing a bank and another guy rifling some company's pension fund. They are both stealing, and the latter scumbag's theft has an even greater impact on society. We had one really slick pension-rifler in our town. Nobody knew a thing about him until he supposedly escaped from the FBI after being arrested and allowed to make one phone call in a local restaurant. Which was okay, because they caught that same guy a year later doing, you guessed it, rifling the pension fund of yet another unsuspecting company. The way I see it, crime is crime. You do some big white-collar crime, you should do some big prison time. Or how about fifteen years in the Peace Corps? Put your butt in a hut.

10-8

So far I haven't popped anybody with my baton...yet. I hope I never have to. I had some faith in those things until an instructor at the police academy said he broke one on some 300-pound woman he was battling with!

10-8

Sometimes when cops party together, they go a little too far. That, "I'm the baddest dude or dudette out there" attitude that we need on the street for the job definitely bleeds over into our party mode. We think we can do just about anything and get away with it. Hey, we're cops. You pump us up with a little alcohol and you'd be absolutely astounded at what can and often does happen. So just be prepared. Usually, not much happens and it's no big deal. But cops in the monster party mode are not a pleasant sight. You don't generally want to be near us. Just stand back, let us act like apes and pay for it the next day with a brutal hangover, and everything will be okay.

10-8

Accidental discharge. You hear it a lot. You see it a lot. A fleeing offender gets plugged in the back of the head. "I dropped my gun and it accidentally went off." Or a cop and some other idiot are in a bar. The idiot gets holed out. Accidental discharge. I wonder sometimes. Don't you have to point and pull the trigger to shoot somebody?

10-8

I feel sorry for the many, many guys out there who want to be cops, who would make good cops, but they can't be, for some reason. It's either a physical problem, a less-than-lily-white past, or trouble with written exams. I've met many guys I know would make good cops, I can just feel it when I talk with them for awhile. But they never will be. And there are lots of cops out there who shouldn't be. Oh, well, nobody said life had to be fair.

10-8

A message to all cops' wives and husbands: I respect you for putting up with so many things. The missed parties, missed social functions, missed family get-togethers, the danger of the job, the limited income, the long hours, the rotating shifts, the political mumbo-jumbo, cop groupies, the frustration. Keep an eye on your cop. Help ease away those frustrations, if you can. Be there for him or her when the nightmare stuff happens. Support them 100%. Don't let them dive into the bottle and stay there. And if they do, try to pull them out. Try not to dwell too long on the negative. Accentuate the positive. If you are a social climber or into keeping up with the Joneses, you probably shouldn't be a cop's wife. If you want to get involved, join an auxiliary league, or start one. I'm surprised at how few there are. If you think your cop is under too much pressure to get promoted or to make overtime, try to take some of the pressure off. Rely on other cops' spouses when times are tough. Only they know what it's like.

10-8

Cop groupies. Yes, they do exist. And I'm here to say that these gals are okay, but more than likely they are bound to be trouble. It's hard to hate people who really dig cops, especially if they're cute. Sometimes it's tough not to get involved. But I've known a few of these gals who have really put the brakes on promising careers. Let's not even mention marriages.

10-8

As a cop, your service weapon is really an awesome responsibility. When you take on the duties that come with the badge, you are vested with the power to use that weapon. We don't fire warning shots anymore. When the pistola gets yanked out, it's meant to be used. And don't forget, lots of cops are killed with their own service guns every year. That missile-launcher that every cop carries is very quiet. It doesn't say much. It doesn't have to. It has the potential to protect, or to kill.

10-8

I guess the fact that our town is situated on a large lake is one reason why we have a swim test as part of the physical-fitness assessment for PD applicants. Back in 1982, when I received notification that I had passed the written exam and was scheduled for the fitness test, I was delighted to learn about the swim test. I was on the swim team in high school. I breezed through the 100-yard swim test and ended up doing quite well on all of the requirements for the fitness portion of the hiring process. The other exercises included pushups, pullups, burpees, a dive into the deep end of the high school swimming pool to retrieve a five-pound rubber brick, a rope climb, situps, carrying another person your weight on your back for twenty yards, and after all that, only a 330-yard run. By the end of the afternoon I felt like I had completed a mini-Olympics.

10-8

Things I carry on my service belt: pistola and holster, two ammo magazines in a holder, radio with holder, handcuff case with handcuffs, baton with ring holder, and four keepers (slim leather snap-straps) that secure my duty belt to my regular pants belt. If you're thinking that sounds like a lot of stuff to be carrying around, you're right. But there are still more items I'd like to be able to carry. Like a small flashlight with holder and a small can of pepper spray in a holder. And let me tell ya, bolting after some scumbag is no cakewalk with all that gear hanging on you.

10-8

If you're dating a cop, be prepared to dig down deep into your well of patience. Social events that are missed, gun-toting dates, that feeling that no matter how close you get you will always be on the outside, maniac cop buddies, the weird (eyes darting everywhere or I've-got-to-sit-facing-the-door) kind of behavior, the worrying, the waiting....It's a pretty long list.

10-8

Do cops drink lots of coffee? You bet! How else are we going to stay alert in order to better protect John Q. Public? And for health reasons, you have to consume copious amounts of donuts to dilute the coffee in the stomach, right?

10-8

Cops, prosecutors, judges, and jurors taking bribes. It happens. After all we and they are only humans, so we're all susceptible to human weakness. A vast majority of us do our work and resist temptation when it happens. Bribes compromise the entire system. Is it worse for a traffic cop to take a few bucks to "loose" a ticket, or for a judge to throw a serious case? I may be prejudiced, but when a judge takes a bribe it's as about serious as it can get.

10-8

So-called expert-witnesses-for-hire are more like mouthpieces-for-money. In some cases, these people are vital to the judicial process, allowing the introduction of a kind of second opinion, or giving a different perspective or angle to important cases, or just getting as much of the plain truth in front of the judge or jury as possible. But I'm sorry to say that in most cases it seems that defense attorneys just shop around until they can find some jerk with a few qualifications who'll testify to anything the defense wants him or her to, as long as the money is right. These people will say anything, including flying in the face of logic and the standards of their own profession, for dough. If these people are good enough, they can fudge a factor here, twist a piece of evidence there, just enough to confuse a judge or jury. Don't get me wrong, this does go both ways. Expert testimony for the prosecution can be prejudiced also. And because the defense deserves it's shot, I don't see any real solutions to this problem of witnesses-for-hire that currently plagues our judicial system. I only hope that judges and juries are sensitive enough to see through some of this testimony.

10-8

When you're a cop, you're bound to have to deal with a few dead people. Maybe a lot. I handle it by trying to think of a body as just what it is. Just that, a body that was once a vessel for some person's soul on its earthly voyage this go-around. Only dead, mortal flesh remains; the real spirit of the person has moved on. That sure makes it easier for me.

10-8

Something cops fear but can do very little about is latent killers. These are people with no love, no support system, and no outlets. They are okay as long as things stay pretty much the same. Then one thing, or maybe even a series of events, sparks a chain reaction that will ultimately push this person toward making a deadly decision. It could be a divorce or the day the divorce becomes final. It could be a birthday, a holiday, or an anniversary. It could be a problem with the job, such as being passed up for promotion or being fired. It could be a problem with a girlfriend or an ex-girlfriend. Or it could be something so subtle that no one else notices, just some diddly, minor thing that breaks open the dam, unleashing a great evil: the conscious decision to kill somebody. In some cases there are warning signs, such as abnormal behavior or threats or harassing phone calls, stalking, or even minor assaults. But many times there are no outward indications at all of the trouble brewing inside. These people do not go around wearing signs saying, *Beware, I'm going to do somebody soon.* So no one can detect or stop them. Innocent people are killed, and it's too late. We're left horrified, crying, putting our heads in our hands, picking up the pieces and asking ourselves why it happened, wishing it never happened, wishing we could have stopped it somehow, looking for someone or something to blame, losing our faith, feeling really helpless, and finally knowing that it will happen again and again. It seems to be happening more and more these days. Witness the two separate shooting incidents in two different post offices that happened just today. I always hope and pray that this kind of thing doesn't happen in our town. Or that either I or someone else in a position to do so will stop it before it happens. Obviously, at times like this, people's thoughts turn to stricter gun control or heavier security measures. With more than 200,000,000 guns already out there, I'm not sure whether either idea contains the answer. We have to look more closely at ourselves for the solution.

10-8

Pray for all the men and women in law enforcement who dedicate their lives to the protection of others, day after day, year after year, decade after decade. Silent heroes.

10-8

Should extended families be held responsible and even liable for the criminal or unjust acts of family members? I don't know about this one, but I believe if this were so, it would force extended families to take a more active interest in the conduct of their black sheep. More assistance would be available for victims of crimes. Closer family ties would be established, and the concept of family honor would be more than just a concept. Heavy and continued familial pressure coupled with support could actually serve to reduce crime. I said *could* on that last one, didn't I? Because there are a few problems with this type of system. I suppose that large families with larger financial holdings— cash, stocks, and real estate—might be able to buy justice. And it's usually the poorer families and that particular environment that foster the really bad criminals. But I'm not sure.

10-8

Is justice equal for everybody in America today? From what I've seen of the system, it appears on the outside to be fair. But when I look and see who is actually in prison doing the hard time, I begin to have my doubts. It doesn't always have to do with race or socio-economic status. In many cases there seems to be a vast difference in sentencing for exactly the same crime from one jurisdiction to another, or from one court system to another, or from one geographic region to another. This is pure speculation on my part. I remember a few years back before I became a cop, when I was driving a limo for a living. I was talking with one of my fares, this really cool black corrections administrator for the State of California, who happened to be attending a conference in my area. I asked him point-blank why there were so many black people in prison. He told me that in his jurisdiction, armed robbery was the crime most often associated with both a high apprehension rate and a long jail sentence. He further related that armed robbery was one of those crimes most often committed by blacks because of their low economic status. So, a lot of blacks were doing it, a lot of them were getting caught, and a lot of them were getting sent to jail for a long time. He went on to quote me a figure for the average amount of cash taken in armed robberies in his jurisdiction for the year 1979 or around that time. I won't forget what it was. Sixty-two dollars! Think about it. Risking the loss of freedom for years of your life for sixty-two bucks. What have we become?

10-8

My greatest fear for the future of our society is that our technology, computers in particular, will so far remove us from nature, and from our natural state, that we will eventually be removed from being human. That most of our basic decisions in the future will not be made by us but by a computer, or that our actions will always be controlled by a computer (think of our entire lives being reduced to little 1s and 0s). That most things will be done for us by technology. That we will be left as a mere collection of spectators outside the workplace and the real, natural world, continuously jacked into TV or VR (virtual reality) to the extent that the real reality, our spiritual relationship with the ground, the sky, the earth, the trees, the flora, and the fauna, and thus our own souls, will cease to exist. Any need will be provided for, through technology, or drugs.

10-8

In that future where our lives our governed by the computer, even with all that control the police will still be around. But the only crimes left to be committed will be thought crimes and anti-norm behavioral crimes. Imagine the kind of technology that will be needed to monitor and detect the former. I envision a society with the technology and the pressure and the lifelessness depicted in the science fiction movie *THX1138*, made by George Lucas, with some of the twisted mind-speak and Big Brother control from *1984* thrown in. And go further with me if you will, to a time when an individual's entire life experiences will be gathered not from real life, but from TV and VR. What would an individual exposed to that kind of input grow up to be like? I'm not sure. I am sure that at least some human dimensions would be totally lacking. I think we are looking at some of that right now with all the violence we are exposed to in the communications media. Sometimes I think, God help us, give me the Ten Commandments and the farm. Except that I'm kind of wild, I'm a night person, and I'm allergic to corn dust and hay. And so far in my life I've had a heck of a time dealing with some of those Commandments. But I still believe I would find much more peace by tilling the fresh earth, by hearing the bird's song and the wind whisper in the trees, by basking in the warm glow of the sun, by feeling the waves lapping over my feet, than by taking some pills and watching it all on TV in some little metal cubicle buried far underground. I know what I have said sounds pretty grim. I hope it never happens. But judging from what I have seen and where I think we're headed, that unnatural future is definitely a possibility. Of course if it were to come to pass, there would be no real criminals. There would be no crime. There would be no freedom. There would be only adjustments.

10-8

I wonder about prison a lot. I'm a wimp when it comes to that convict stuff. I shiver every time I take a gander at one of our cells at the PD. I say a silent prayer that I will never end up languishing away in some cell. But knowing myself and today's world, it seems possible that I could end up in the "Graybar Hotel," another sorry statistic. That's just a feeling I have; no real explanation for it. So I think about our prisoners. I think about the people on death row. Is it worse for them, waiting to die like that? Or do those people greet each new day with eagerness and relief? I don't know, I've never been in prison. During my lifetime, I've done some things I probably could have gone to prison for. I've never felt what it's like to be sentenced to die or to live for the rest of my life in jail. But it could be said that we are all incarcerated in our own kind of prison, prisoners of our own false beliefs and fears. And that as human beings we all live under a death sentence. I think I know where real freedom comes from. It comes from the mind. It's in the mind, man.

10-8

Recently I sat dumbfounded as I watched a TV news special focusing on two coppers from a major metropolitan city in this country, brazenly spilling their guts in front of some special investigations committee. It was absolutely chilling to watch fellow cops arrogantly admitting to some really serious crimes perpetrated by them while on the job. It made me sick and stunned the members of the committee. Folks, you have no idea what temptation there is out there for honest cops to do wrong.

10-8

How's this for a lovely domestic violence situation? Mom is drunk, Dad is drunk, they've got three small kids, and Mom and Dad are so pissed off at each other that they can't stay under the same roof. Great, just great!

10-8

Not too long ago I received a very sweet card from the concerned parents of a guy I arrested. They mailed it to the police station to thank me for doing my job. First time in my career this has happened! The love and concern and sensitivity shown in this brief message are an encouragement and an inspiration to me.

10-8

No-driving days. We should have those. One or two Sundays a month if you don't hoof it or pedal it or sail it or skate it or kite it, you don't go anywhere. Emergency vehicles only. Let's just give the roads and our lungs and our peace of mind a break, okay?

10-8

I get very red in the face when defense attorneys and their guilty clients yammer on and on about the right to drive. Let me make this perfectly clear. There is no such thing as the "right" to drive. Driving a motor vehicle is a *licensed privilege*. ALL drivers who take to the roadways are entrusted with the lives, property, and safety of others. Motor vehicles have the potential to cause great harm if used improperly. In order to get a license you have to practice driving, study the rules of the road, and pass a written exam and maybe even a driving exam. Then once you have that license in your hot little hands, you actually have to pretty much follow the rules and regs out there on the road. If you don't, then you deserve to lose your license. Driving is not a right like the right to free speech or the right to peaceably assemble. Everyone who takes to the highways of our fair land has the right to be surrounded by careful, experienced, skillful, concerned drivers. To me, possessing a driver's license is the same thing as having a pilot's license. There's no difference. So don't be a hazard out there. And don't give me that right-to-drive stuff.

10-8

Alcohol abuse. A serious, serious problem. Health problems, mental problems, job problems, family problems, all can be caused or aggravated by alcohol abuse. Alcoholism cuts across all age, racial, economic, and gender groups. Many, many serious crimes and major personal setbacks can be tied directly to alcohol abuse. Countless homicides, rapes, assaults, abuses of children and spouses, fatal or serious car accidents, domestic disputes, lost jobs, suicides, divorces, hospitalizations, and "natural" deaths can be attributed to alcohol abuse. Millions of lives have been lost in that battle with the bottle. And alcohol is a poison, for God's sake; it's toxic. So what do we do? Prohibition didn't work. It merely funneled huge amounts of untaxed cash into the wrong hands. I lean more toward greater awareness, counseling, and support programs. But programs cost money. I personally could do with a few fewer cruise missiles. Nonalcoholic beers are certainly a step in the right direction. Cars that won't start unless the operator is under the legal limit work for me. But before we can successfully lick alcoholism, we have to determine the underlying causes for its proliferation in this country. I'm going with general depression and lack of adventure. It sounds naive, but I think if we were busier and felt more like we were contributing, we would drink less. But I'm no expert. I don't even know the definition of an alcoholic.

10-8

Peepholes on exterior doors. A very good idea. You have a solid exterior door. Somebody knocks on that door. A nice peephole with a fisheye lens and an exterior light will allow you to eyeball who is at your door, so you don't let in Mr. Badguy. A peephole in that rear metal door of your business wouldn't be such a bad idea, either. It could very well keep you from getting robbed. They don't cost much and they are relatively easy to install.

10-8

Guys who carry large amounts of cash around are either very insecure, very busy, or very stupid. Guys who carry a lot of cash around and flash it all the time are suicidal. I don't care how bad you think you are, there is always somebody out there who is badder. You'll find out, too. So just carry what you need. Stash some in the car or in your socks, whatever. I carry my wallet in my *front* pocket. I don't know if it helps me or not, but there are pickpockets out there. They're slick, and they use accomplices to bump you or otherwise divert your attention from what they are busy doing, which is lifting your wallet.

10-8

I know it's a bitch, but there would be no such thing as an honest, fair, and impartial police department without some kind of taxation.

10-8

Police brutality and excessive use of force, or necessary use of force? Sensitive issue. So let's get right to it. Most people don't understand the cop job. They are totally unaware or don't want to face the fact that for cops to do their jobs effectively, the threat of violence or even brutal force on the part of cops must always be present. To prevent crimes, to prevent assaults, to prevent disorderly conduct, I've gotta tell you, scumbags must be shown or taught that if they screw up or don't comply, they're gonna get their asses kicked. As I said before, we have to be the baddest out there. We must win in every or almost every situation to be effective on the street. And I'm here to tell you, sometimes the line between necessary and excessive force gets real blurry.

10-8

Racial violence. Religious violence. Ethnic violence. It sure seems like a lot of violence is going around. Just reading the Bible will tell you that this kind of behavior is not new to humanity. It has probably been with us ever since man discovered he could use a word or a gesture or a rock or a club against his fellow man. More and more these days, I hear people talking about some radical "solutions:" genocide...separation...ethnic cleansing. Some actually suggest that we just divvy up the old U.S. of A.; what's left of the American Indians will get some of the Great Plains, blacks will get some of the South, Asians will get some of the West, Hispanics will get some of the Southwest, and white folks will get what's left over. But we'd still grouse and fight over what we have and what we think we need, because nobody would be satisfied with what they had, and we'd be right back to square one. I still lean toward an understanding through education. What makes this country great is its diversity. But diversity without understanding and education causes problems. People naturally fear and may even resent what they don't understand. I say we keep the diversity while encouraging free thinking and cooperation. But, hey, I'm just a cop and these are just the ramblings of a cop, okay?

10-8

There are more homicides involving victims under the age of fifteen in the City of Chicago than the total number of the homicides in England. One lousy age group in one city versus an entire nation! This is a shocking statistic. Perhaps we should take a really good look at what the Brits are doing in their society. Or what we are doing wrong.

10-8

We had some really bold burglars whose MO was to go in through the front door of a house and burgle the place while the homeowners were out in the backyard!

10-8

Private security is an absolutely necessary extension of the cop job in this day and age. Sometimes if you want or need special protection, it pays to buy it yourself. Large manufacturing firms, banks, hospitals, schools, condo associations, apartment complexes, parking garages, ports, casinos, resorts, bars, hotels, office buildings, auto dealerships, the list goes on. No way can we regular cops keep an eye on *all* that stuff. That's where private security comes in. Guys or gals with a little training, good knowledge of the layout, a few good TV monitors, good lighting, and a portable radio can really make a big difference in deterring crime in areas where cops just can't be all the time. Did I mention giving these people some decent guns, if needed?

10-8

Construction companies and contractors, marking and painting your tools in a special manner with your logo or your name would not bother me. Nor would I mind if you kept records of models and makes and serial numbers. As a matter of fact, anybody can purchase a low-cost metal scribe that will effectively mark just about any metal object. If a guy steals your hammer and we catch him, your name, initials or, even better, your special mark inscribed on that hammer would make life a lot easier.

10-8

The elderly are often targets for many types of crimes. Con men and women play upon their isolation and helplessness. Some typical scams include fake home inspections; driveway coating schemes; unnecessary and expensive plumbing, heating, or electrical installations; Ponzi let-me-invest-your-money schemes; bogus real estate deals; money-drop scams, and just plain overcharging in general. Beware of strangers who come to your door and ask to come inside.

Beware of telephone tricksters. Do not let anyone inside your home unless you know them, they have a reference, or they are listed in the phone book and can be verified. Ask for references from contractors whom you don't know and check them out. Swallow your pride a little and have a relative or a friend help you with your financial dealings. Remember to keep your valuables in a safe place, preferably not out in the open. And no matter what any stranger or marginal relative says, do not let anyone talk you into going down to your bank, withdrawing your savings, and handing it over for safekeeping.

10-8

To all the people who own real estate in my town, I say thank you. Thank you because every time you held your whopping real estate tax bill in your hand, you grumbled, you swore, and maybe you protested, but at least you paid it. Your steadfastness and support for your city has kept food on the table and a roof overhead for me and my family. I also thank you for not beefing me when my conduct, for one reason or another, was not 100% professional while I was on-duty. And for those in town who did beef me, I despise you for doing it, but I probably deserved it some of the time anyway. I will freely admit that I am not the perfect policeman at all times. But I want you to know that when I'm on-duty you can rely on me to be there when you need me. I am always trying to do the job right. Please give me credit for trying.

10-8

Let's face it, some old folks out there are deadly behind the wheel. They either get into too many accidents or they cause too many accidents. My idea is that any driver over seventy years old who gets into three accidents or gets three traffic tickets in one year says goodbye to that driver's license and hello to that taxicab.

10-8

Crime. Crime. How do we reduce crime? I don't know, to tell you the truth. Cutting off people's hands is probably not the way to go. Harsher prison sentences? I'm not sure that works. How about people just being smarter with their stuff, not piling it all in one place or not letting it hang out there where some perp can swipe it, you know, reducing that window of opportunity. And I truly wish that everybody had a fabulous home to live in, a nice car, a loving, supportive family, and a good job. I'm sure that would greatly reduce crime. But I don't see that happening any time very soon. We're finally realizing that only a very small percentage of the general population is committing a major portion of crimes. Identifying those people is not very hard to do. Figuring out what to do with those people is. The nation's total jail and prison population stands at 1,400,000! One out of every 185 people in America is locked up. That is a tremendous waste of human resources, especially when we are facing so many other difficult issues.

10-8

It's easy to take shots at serial killers. They scare the hell out of me and everyone else. They represent a great evil that has taken root; I mean it's not just visiting, it's here to stay in those people. Whatever it is that produces these sociopathic monsters, be it chemical imbalance, a twisted childhood, or a twisted adulthood, the results are always the same. Innocent people are murdered, leaving the rest of us shocked and horrified. I think captured serial killers should be studied in great detail, their dirty secrets pried out of their sick minds and used by law enforcement to catch other serial killers or to prevent future needless slayings. And you already know my feelings on capital punishment. I get really perturbed when I wonder if the frequency of serial killings is a barometer for how our society is progressing. If this is true, we are in real trouble.

10-8

A quick way to reduce motor vehicle accidents, thus saving lives, preventing injuries, and preserving property, is to lower speed limits, *everywhere*. Speed kills. Hey, I don't like driving slow, either. I'm just throwing this out there for consideration. Do we really need to be in such a hurry?

10-8

Folks, please keep the serial numbers of all your stuff that has a serial number on it in a handy place. Because if it gets stolen and it isn't marked, how are we supposed to tell if it's your stuff or not?

10-8

There are two kinds of police patrol: reactive and proactive. Reactive patrol is when we just drive around and roll on a call only after it comes into the PD. Proactive patrol is when the cops really use their brains, plan ahead, and are in the right place at the right time to either nab the bad guy or thwart the crime before it ever goes down. Anybody can be reactive, but proactive is the way to go. Take it from me, an ounce of proactive is worth a ton of reactive, any day of the week!

10-8

So, you've finally come to the decision that you want to be a cop. That alone tells me something. Either you really have it all together and you have family members in the job already or you are a total blathering idiot, running around saying things like, "I just want to help people" and "I want to lock those scumbags up and throw away the key." I'll tell you how it happened with me. Frankly, I needed the money. I needed a job that paid all right and had some benefits. Now that I have the job, I do get satisfaction from helping people and locking the bad guys up. But let's forget about me for a second. How do *you* get started in your pursuit of the cop job? You could scan the papers and just go out and take some police exams and hope for the best. How about taking some criminal justice courses? How about joining an Explorer Post affiliated with a local police department? How about requesting a ride-along with a real cop? I did that, and I got a lot out of it. How about getting into good physical condition, so that you'll be ready for the fitness portion of any police department hiring process? When you're ready, just do what I said, go through word of mouth with your cop friends or keep an eyeball on the want ads, fill out some applications, and take some written exams. Most cops do take more than one test before they get hired on. Oh, I forgot one thing. How about keeping your nose clean by not being with the wrong people at the wrong time or in the wrong place at the wrong time doing the wrong thing?

How about getting over that first hurdle in your quest by accepting another position in a local PD, like dispatcher, community services officer, records clerk? Or how about just picking up a phone and calling your dad, the chief of police, and saying, "Gee Dad, life for me has no meaning or purpose and seems kind of stupid and dull up to now. Can I be a cop, Dad, huh Dad, huh?" Don't laugh, this happens all the time. Hopefully, if you're the right kind of person and you're determined enough, you'll get hired on somewhere, you'll make a contribution, and you'll put some scumbags who deserve it behind bars. You have my best wishes, and my condolences.

10-8

You wave to me while I'm driving around in the squad, I'm going to wave back. You could be a burglar or you could have just killed your wife, I'm still gonna wave back. Unless I'm feeling really surly that day.

10-8

As far as parking tickets go, I look at it this way. A vehicle parked in a no-parking area for a few minutes can always be moved if there is a person in the car. But at any other time, it is fair game. I do need a few things first, before I write a ticket. I need good, clear signage that is posted where it can be seen. And I need a little time, too. I don't just pounce on cars the second after the driver runs into the store or building. To be fair, I wait a minimum of five minutes. But once I start writing out the parking ticket, it's beyond the point of no return. Even if the motorist runs out and says, "I'm moving the car right now," it's too late. Only a judge can cancel a parking ticket, and I don't feel like asking, okay?

10-8

A surefire way to keep it from raining on my shift is for me to bring my raincoat with me, at the beginning of the shift. This works almost every time. And I can't count the number of times I've gotten wet when I didn't bring the damned thing.

10-8

Another thing that really pisses me off: Every once in a while, some judge will fly directly into the face of all logic, reason, sanity, and precedents and burp up some cockamamie ruling that lets some guilty scumbag off the hook. The really bad part is when all these defense attorneys scurry around like lemmings to jump on the bandwagon and try to get their obviously guilty clients off for the same thing, lending huge credence to some totally ridiculous, abnormal ruling.

10-8

One midnight shift I caught this twenty-five-year-old kid trying to get into one of our specialty auto dealerships out on the highway. I arrested him and took him down to the PD. His criminal history showed one count of burglary, so the assistant state's attorney who was on call that night authorized a serious charge of attempted burglary for my guy. Before I locked him up, I asked him if he wanted to call home. He said no. So in the morning he was taken before a judge in bond court and, because he had a criminal record and couldn't make bail, he got locked up in the county jail. The next time I saw the kid was a week later. I was up in court on an unrelated matter when my guy was brought into that particular courtroom for a status hearing. The change in him was dramatic. He'd been very cooperative with me, but he apparently didn't take to jail too well. Before the judge, he was handcuffed (very rare), leg manacled (I'd never seen this before), surrounded by four beefy deputies, and he looked like a maniac. I learned that since the day he got up to the county jail he had fought continuously with other inmates and guards. I ran into his mother outside the courtroom. She told me that her son was mentally handicapped and had probably been looking for his deceased father who used to work in a small car dealership. I'm not sure I believe her entire story, but I felt bad because just one phone call could have prevented a lot of suffering.

10-8

Holograms. Fascinating technology. Allowing us to view a facsimile of any object as a three-dimensional projection from any angle. I say we holo criminals good, real good, and then broadcast that image all over the place.

10-8

Patronizing local businesses. Local cops going to local shops. The barber, the tailor, the restaurants, the appliance stores, whatever. Not for the discount, but for the *support*, the rapport with the local business community.

10-8

Some police departments tie traffic enforcement levels in with pay increases. The more tickets a cop writes, the more money he or she makes. That's bullshit. We shouldn't be made to write tickets. We should be allowed to make our own choices and to use our own discretion on the street. We shouldn't be forced to alter our standards just for dough. When I write somebody a ticket it's because he or she did something wrong and did it in such a way that I think it's bad enough to be penalized for it.

10-8

We had this local kid who was kind of a character. One day he was standing in a long line at the local supermarket waiting to buy a pack of cigarettes. Well, the line was too long, and he didn't want to wait. So he just bolted out of the store without paying for the cigarettes. We had a copper right in the area at the time of the call, and he chased this kid for about half a mile before losing him. I just happened to be driving around in the parking lot of a nearby church when this kid charged out of some bushes, ran to the front of my squad, threw the cigarettes on the ground, put his hands on the hood and said, "Okay, you got me. I stole the cigarettes because I didn't want to wait in line." It was one of my first pinches, and one of my easiest. All over a pack of cigarettes. When the other cop who'd chased him found out how I pinched our "thief," he was really pissed.

10-8

One time we got called to the scene of this domestic disturbance on the south side of town. This guy and gal who'd been living together for two years finally decided to get married that day. Well, the groom drank too much, threw stuff around in the house, and threw his brand new wife around. This guy was uncontrollable. We didn't arrest him. Instead we took him to a local hotel to sleep it off, because we all understood about the marriage thing, all of us who responded having been married twice. A domestic on your first day of marriage. Not good.

10-8

We have three commuter train stations in our city limits and sometimes I like to drive by them in the middle of the evening rush hour just to watch the people's faces to see if they're happy or not when they get off the train. These are the winners, the guys and gals with the good, professional jobs in the city who can afford the big houses, the expensive cars, the manicured lawns and kids and dogs and spouses. I scrutinize the expressions on their faces and examine the kinds of clothes they wear and the way they walk. I want to see them happy, confident. They seem okay for the most part. The men wear the expensive, conservative suits and the women favor the power wardrobe. I tried the commuting thing downtown one time. Taking the train to the big city, walking to my job in that glass tower in the sky behind some desk with the phone in my ear all day, and then taking the train home. I went totally bonkers in three days! Oh, well. My father and his father did it for years. I guess I'm just cut out for something different.

10-8

I suppose you already know about the mass migration that occurs every week in our country. The emigres are our own children! A divorce rate hovering somewhere around 50% has ushered a large sector of America into a shuttling phenomenon that has received some study but very little attention. Because nobody wants to talk about it, and nobody wants to face it, and nobody wants to consider the damage done by it. To put it plainly, child custody decrees force helpless children to make a weekly and sometimes daily trek from the world of one parent to the world of another. The children in these cases must, in essence, "work their own shifts." These shifts involve two things. One is to witness the constant, forced contact between the divorced parents who have already decided that they don't want to see each other any more. The other is the yo-yoing of the poor kids between two lives that in all likelihood are as diametrically opposed as the divorced parents themselves. That has to be tough. I only hope that the divorced parents can be as gentle and truthful as possible with their children. At the same time I hope that our children are smart enough to understand why this stuff has to happen to them. Child custody exchanges are fraught with emotion, even in the mildest divorces. And by the way, let me say that as a divorced parent I count myself as a participant in this cycle.

10-8

One time this woman called the PD and wanted us to send our public works guys out to search the sewers around her house for a bottle of perfume that she lost down the drain. Give us a break, lady. Call a plumber for God's sake if you want to find it that badly.

10-8

Let me tell you the story of what I call "The Child Custody Dispute from Hell." Imagine, if you will, a nice, sunny, summer Sunday afternoon. Peaceful. Then you and the unlucky copper in the beat next to yours get sent to a very nice house in a very quiet neighborhood, reference a possible problem with a custody exchange that is to occur there. Then imagine you and your shiftmate pulling up to the front of the residence, sitting in your squads for about five minutes, and just when you're wiping your brow and saying, "Phew, I guess we dodged the bullet on this one" and you're getting ready to split, the fuse is suddenly lit, and the bomb explodes in your faces. The fuse is two cars pulling up to the curb in front of the house. A big Mercedes and another big Mercedes. This is not good. This means big bucks, with backup. Mom exits first car and storms to the front door of residence. Mom's sister and brother-in-law get out of second vehicle, march up to front door of residence, and take up a defensive stance behind Mom. At that precise moment, Mom's twelve-year-old son rides up the street on his bike, scopes out the situation, decides to split. Mom and support forces never get fully into position, because the front door of the residence explodes outward and Dad, who I'm sure at one time was a sane and reasonable guy, is now a 6'1", 200-pound maniac. He rushes out doing the gorilla thing, screaming and threatening the sister-in-law, who has probably pumped so much acid into Dad over the divorce that Dad doesn't care about Mom but wants to strangle the sister instead. Well, I can't let him do that. So I do the low-profile thing and grab his right arm (hoping he is a right-handed strangler) and just hold on. My backup, meanwhile, is keeping an even lower profile by not doing anything at all. Thanks a lot. Now picture this dandy little scene. Dad is stalking sister-in-law all over the front yard, meanwhile flinging me around like a rag doll, my hat is falling off, and everybody is yelling. What could be worse? It gets worse. Dad's really foxy-looking, younger female live-in jocker chooses this precise moment to make an entrance by stepping out of the front door, oh so casually, creating a new focus for even more screaming invective. But don't stop there. Have the two young daughters come out from the house and start crying their little eyes out. Great, just great. Jesus, I'm thinking as I'm being tossed all over the place, will this ever end? Yes, I'm happy to say that it finally did end. Final upshot: We called the supervisor. When the shit hits the fan, that's what we do, call the supervisor. He arrived in all his white-shirt, gold-star, gold-stripe splendor, and even though he was a total idiot, he made the right call. A punt. Sorry folks, but even though Mom is brandishing some kind of court order in her hot little hand, we can't enforce it. It's the county sheriff's jurisdiction. We let the kids decide where to go for right now. Older sister and brother (who returned to the scene looking mighty sheepish) surprisingly elected to stay with Dad and his girl-friend, which made me look at Mom kinda funny. Youngest daughter, who is about three, decided to go home with Mommy. I picked up my hat and slinked away, thinking to myself, Did that really just happen? I hope nobody saw it!

10-8

How about a reversal rule for all those bullshit lawsuits floating around in our courts these days? As a cop, I get stuck in the middle of a few of them every now and then. Unscrupulous people with their unscrupulous attorneys should be made to pay big bucks in damages to the people they are suing when such lawsuits are found to be frivolous or totally unwarranted. Theoretically I know this is possible, but I never hear of it happening. Hey, I know there are some serious grievances out there that need to be redressed, but this other stuff has gotten way out of hand.

10-8

Cooperation. Joint operations. Networking. Law enforcement agencies working *together*. That's the way to go. But traditionally, sharing information is not an easy thing for cops to do, even if it means putting the bad guy away quicker. We naturally prefer to arrest everybody ourselves, and thus we hold our own cards pretty close to our vests. That's just the way we are. Even in my own department, very little information is shared between the road cops and the detective bureau or even between one shift and another. Don't even mention between one department and another. Although all the towns near us share the same type of crimes and the same criminals, we never get together to discuss strategies or to share information. Not once a month, not once a year, not once in a blue moon. You'd think meetings like this would be beneficial. But who am I to say?

10-8

We're cops. We're not gods. We have a job to do. Please, please cooperate with us. If we happen to stop you and ask you for your name and what you are doing or for some identification, don't give us a hard time. We're doing it for a reason. Make life easier for everybody. And don't lie, okay? Because when you do we know it, and then we get really mad.

10-8

There are many ways to resist a cop. You could simply refuse to give us your name or any information when we ask you. You could refuse to do what we say. You could actively, physically resist being arrested by pushing or kicking or hitting or biting or shooting or stabbing. You could passively resist by just lying on the ground and making it hard for us to handcuff you. Or you could just run away. However you resist, expect trouble. Because we won't put up with it. No way. I won't attack anyone who is passively resisting. We'll just have our little wrestling match and be done with it. But you push me or take a pop at me or run from me, you're going to get it, either from me or me and a few other cops. And watch your passive resisting. To a lot of cops, resisting is resisting and you are going to get roughed up, whether you're passively resisting or actively resisting.

10-8

We just started a bicycle patrol with real coppers this summer. One guy has already arrested a drunk driver while biking it around our business district. That cop gets an A-plus from me.

10-8

I had a very brief relationship with one of our dispatchers. I was with her for a total of about four hours over a three-week period before I figured out that we really weren't a match. You live and learn. But it's kind of goofy because we have to work together all the time. I probably shouldn't have done it, but I thought we had something. I guess in this case the imagining and the kidding around were more fun than the commitment part.

10-8

The other day a convicted child kidnapper and molester who was wanted in connection with yet another case ran head-on into a semi while being chased by the police. He ended up in a few parts. I wonder if the guy decided to take justice into his own hands.

10-8

This is the story of two parades. Twice each year I get assigned to work traffic control for parades in our town. The contrast between the two parades is stunning and conveys its own message. The first parade is the Memorial Day parade. The cops assigned to this parade always outnumber the participants, and the spectators, too for that matter. No bands, no drums, no bugles, no fanfare, just eight or ten guys marching around for about ten minutes in the business district, wearing their old military uniforms and carrying a flag. But the poignancy and solemnity of the moment when these few proud, quiet men pass by my post never fails to put a huge lump in my throat. Compare this to the Fourth of July parade. Huge turnout, multiple bands, five full blocks of kids and pets, drum corps, flag corps, Scouts, clowns, fire engines, squad cars, Shriners, politicians, local business-men, antique cars, an hour and a half of who-knows-what-next. It took me awhile to figure it out, but I now know the difference between the two parades. In the Fourth of July parade, we celebrate our freedom and ourselves by what we decreed with words way back in 1776. On Memorial Day, we remember how that freedom was paid for, in deeds and in lives.

10-8

The other night a copper on my shift found a woman's purse and shoes in a park down by the lake. The owner of those items was found two days later, about three miles out. I've often wondered what exactly goes through people's minds when they are about to commit suicide. I hope I never find out.

10-8

One of the police stations in our area took a direct hit by lightning the other night. The strike blew out their radio communications for a short while. Now that's scary.

10-8

We have this defense attorney who represents some of the real clas-sic scumbags in our area. Which is not unusual in itself. But this guy used to be a cop from the nearby town where I grew up. What kind of mind-set do you have to have to make a career change like that? I know he's not the first to do it. He won't be the last, either.

10-8

Last night when I went back in to work after my days off, there were three more of those teletype messages taped to the wall behind the communications desk. Three law enforcement officers from different parts of the country were killed in the last three weeks by suspects who used the coppers' own service weapons. These messages get taped to the wall so we can read and grieve, but mostly so we can learn from the fatal mistakes made by our fallen comrades in a "war" that never ends.

10-8

One time I got dispatched to this business in our town out on the highway, reference a suspicious subject. It was about 5:00 in the afternoon on a cold, wet, rainy day. The suspicious subject turned out to be a well-developed white male about seventeen years of age, running around in his underwear. Nobody knew who he was or where he came from. He was a good-looking kid, although he was mentally handicapped and could not speak. He was obviously very frightened. I had to chase him around for a while and I was surprised by the feral strength he possessed. He was small in stature, about 5' 6", weighing about 140, but his strength and vitality impressed me. Holding him was like holding a deer. Somebody finally came and picked him up.

10-8

One time I arrested a pretty bad dude for driving under the influence of drugs. He had a theft warrant from another town. This guy was only twenty-two years old, but already had an impressive number of arrests for armed robbery, including a four-year stint in prison. We talked a lot, but I didn't have enough time with him to learn why he had done all those robberies. I try to look for good qualities in everyone. Even this guy had a warm side to him. If only that side had been nurtured, instead of the other, darker side, things might have turned out differently for this guy.

10-8

Bad weather. A cop can't hide from it. You are stuck out there, doing your thing in extreme cold, extreme heat, extreme rain, and tons and tons of snow. We're even better than the mailman. We're always out there, no matter what Mother Nature has in store, because we have to be.

10-8

Sometimes you can wait just a little bit too long before arresting a drunk driver. One night I was following this guy southbound on the highway. He was weaving a little and he couldn't seem to keep his speed very constant, but it was 2:30 in the morning and maybe he was just tired. I was going to stop him, but there's no hurry, right? Wrong. At the very next intersection, the guy almost impaled himself on the front end of the concrete median. At the last second, he yanked the wheel to the right and narrowly avoided being killed. I stopped him immediately after that little number, and he ended up blowing a big number, a .26.

10-8

One time the administration assigned me to directed drunk-driver patrol for one month; 7:00 at night to 3:00 in the morning. Final score: me 23, drunk drivers 0. But I got a little burned out. Despite my zeal for nabbing drunk drivers, I was glad when the month was over.

10-8

This year the second-to-last entrant in the Fourth of July parade was a Scottish bagpipe band. The final entrant was a black rifle-and-flag corps boombox-shimmy-knock-'em-dead kind of thing. Quite a juxtaposition. I loved it. It reminded me that our nation is really a stew pot of many wildly different cultures. We're all in the same parade, but it sure is nice to be proud of our heritages and to let our culture hang out every once in a while.

10-8

Sometimes as a cop you can find yourself in some pretty ridiculous situations. Like thirty feet up a tree trying to coax an uncooperative cat into a laundry basket on a hot, muggy Sunday afternoon. At times like that, you have to stop and think to yourself, *What the hell am I doing?*

10-8

Several times I've had arrestees jettison their little drug stash right in front of me. Sometimes I let them get away with it because I just don't care. If they want to ruin their lives with drugs abuse, then so be it. But sometimes I get pissed, pick up whatever it is off the ground, and charge them with possession.

10-8

There's this monster who shot and killed and mutilated three innocent young women. He gets free room, three square meals a day, is allowed to play softball, and doesn't have to work, all for the rest of his life. Now you tell me, what in the hell is wrong with this picture?

10-8

Once in a while I have to testify in front of a grand jury in order to get some scumbag charged with a felony. Felonies are potentially very serious, jail-time stuff. Just charging a suspect with a felony involves a review of the case by an assistant state's attorney, an indictment drafted by the assistant state's attorney, and either a grand-jury hearing or a formal felony hearing in front of a judge. All that just to charge somebody and bring him to trial. Grand-jury hearings are very brief and usually to the point. If the charging cop has to answer more than five or six questions, the hearing has gone too long. The grand jury itself is made up of anywhere between sixteen and twenty people. Just plain folks. They have to sit and listen carefully to an unending procession of cops and detectives talking about how they found this or that drug or how so-and-so did such-and-such and was identified by this or that means. It can get pretty tedious, but grand-jury work is essential to the process. The information has to be reviewed by somebody who is impartial.

10-8

Not too long ago some idiot ate an ounce of cocaine while being arrested, to avoid prosecution. The ruse worked; he was never brought to trial on possession charges. That's because he refused any medical attention, which wouldn't have helped him anyway, and he died.

10-8

Shift work. I find myself thinking more and more about it lately. Twenty years of this shit. I don't know if I can do it, make the twenty. Sometimes I can feel myself aging at an accelerated rate, especially on the midnight shift. I think about getting a regular day job. But for right now I've got obligations, so I just put up with it and hope for the best.

10-8

The bad guys don't always succeed. One morning about 4:30 we got this call from a jogger who'd seen something very suspicious in the loading dock area of this local theme park. It turned out to be the safe from the park's office. It was just sitting there. In what was evidently a bungled inside job, the would-be safecrackers managed to compromise the alarm system but failed to get into the safe itself. There was one hole drilled into the safe. When they realized that they couldn't get into it, the jerks just wheeled the thing out of the office and onto the loading dock. Their contingency plan went awry when they figured out that shoving a 2,000-pound safe off the top of the dock down into the trunk of their getaway car would rapidly turn the vehicle into a fixed object, so they just left the safe there. And there was $20,000 dollars cash in it!

10-8

There's this guy in town I've known for ten years. I know he's a hardworking guy with a little alcohol problem. Life hasn't been too easy for Tom. The other night I caught him driving really drunk. I could have public-assisted him to his house, but I arrested him instead. He now gets counseling and goes to AA meetings. I still see him all the time. I hope he doesn't resent me for arresting him. I hope he straightens out.

10-8

Almost all of my immediate supervisors are chickenshits when it comes to drunk-driving arrests. They're all into this cover-your-ass, jumbo-jet's-gonna-fall-on-the-hospital-any-moment kind of a thing. In actuality, not too damn much happens on midnights in our town. And if something does go down, I know I can always lock my arrestee up temporarily and respond to a call from the station. It's not that big a deal. And they're afraid that if I arrest somebody, they're gonna have to maybe make a decision or something, or sign an I-bond. I've had supervisors come on my traffic stops and make me let people who are drunk go. I've had supervisors at the beginning of a midnight shift tell me straight out not to arrest anybody and to "stay out of trouble." I've had supervisors assign me to certain beats that have less traffic and more businesses to check just to keep me from arresting drunks. These tactics just piss me off and make me try harder.

10-8

Kids, watch out when you've had a little to drink and you feel like goofing around. The other night a guy jumped up onto the back of his girlfriend's car. She started to drive away and he fell onto the roadway, striking his head. He died a few days later. Tragedy can lurk mighty close when you're horsing around like that. So please, try to stay cool.

10-8

One time I stopped this cute little seventeen-year-old for speeding on the highway. She was going 72 in a 55 at 5:30 on a Friday morning. She was coming from the big city, headed back to her small town. She had one speeding conviction already, seven tattoos, and some alcohol on board. She was just one of those gals who gets bored easily and just has to break out every once in awhile. If she was my daughter, I wouldn't know what to do or say. Just be careful out there. Go on and have your fun, but please honey, use a little common sense, okay?

10-8

I'm like a great white shark out there. The bar or the party where you're drinking is on an island. You have to take to the water sometime to get back home to the mainland. Somewhere out there between you and the shore, hidden beneath those calm, sparkling waters, I'm lurking, waiting, gliding powerfully along. When you least expect it, I'll be zooming up from behind, and before you know it I'll take a huge bite out of you. So be smart.

10-8

How's this for fair? This one guy got caught for DUI twice while his driver's license was suspended. The second time he got four months in jail. I arrested a drug dealer who had a little coke, a beeper, a portable telephone, and $2,000 cash on him. This guy was on probation for a previous drug-related offense. He did not go to jail for even one day.

10-8

The other night I arrested Mr. Nope. He was weaving a little and couldn't drive at a steady speed, so I put a traffic stop on him. His speech was slurred and his eyes were red. I could smell alcohol on his breath, so I asked him to step out of his vehicle. That was the last thing he did for me. I asked if he could say the alphabet. "Nope." I asked if he could stand on one leg. "Nope." I asked if he could walk a straight line. "Nope." I asked if he had a driver's license. "Nope." I found an old traffic ticket in his wallet for DUI, and when I ran the number on the ticket it came back that the guy was still suspended for DUI. Did I let him get back in his car and drive away? Nope! Did I stick him with DUI and driving while suspended? Yup!

10-8

We had this local kid who decided to play big shot and do the drug-dealing, gangbanging kind of thing. Soon he accumulated about eight or nine traffic tickets while tooling around with his ignorant buddies in his little red Mustang. So now he can play big shot on foot.

10-8

We had this poor little gal in town for awhile who was beyond Pluto, I mean way out there. Which wouldn't be so bad, except her quirks almost always put her up against the law. She threatened one cop with a paring knife at the police station. She slammed a framed painting over the head of yet another unfortunate officer at the hospital. She used to set fires in her jail cell. The list goes on. Last I heard she was locked up permanently in a rubber room somewhere. The really sad thing is that it wasn't her fault. You see, her mother died when this gal was only a teenager, so she had to play mom to the rest of the family. And wife to her father, in all ways. All ways. That's heavy damage. Her life was ruined, and the real culprit is still free.

10-8

Some cops have a way with women. We've got this one guy who's been on for years. He's a huge, teddy-bear type. Not a rocket scientist by any means. But man, get him near any woman! It's something to watch. I don't know exactly how he does it, but just by using his size and his body language alone, he's a magnet. Once he says about three or four words, women are falling at his feet. Dear God, please shave off a few of my IQ points and lay this guy's gift on me, okay?

10-8

One evening this van I was tailing drove up over a curb, so I put a stop on it. There were two drunks inside. The owner, who was in the front passenger seat, told me he was teaching his buddy how to drive. His buddy had no license and ended up blowing a .17. I told the van owner that it really wasn't the right time to be giving driving lessons.

10-8

Drug legalization. A tough, tough issue. Should we continue or even step up our current no-tolerance policy? Should we bust everything in sight, hand down more harsh prison sentences, confiscate property, et cetera? I'm not so sure. So far, from my point of view, this doesn't seem to be working. For every dealer we bust, there are many more individuals ready to creep out of the woodwork and fill the gap. And I don't see things improving anytime soon. I see a lot of bucks going into the wrong pockets, sort of like the Al Capone thing, when he made $275,000,000 in one year from bootleg liquor sales. I see a lot of lost tax dollars that could be spent on education and drug awareness and drug-abuse programs. All because certain people feel they have the right to tell other people they can't smoke the leaves of a plant that grows naturally everywhere. I don't use drugs. *I am not encouraging drug use.* But I am encouraging the development and deployment of certain innovative, common-sense solutions to basic problems. Some drugs could be legalized, produced, sold, taxed, and regulated. As a trial, just a trial. Or drugs could be mass produced and just given away. I know this stuff sounds drastic. But we have a drastic problem. Just look around you.

10-8

It's a damned strange feeling to be driving home from work in the morning when everybody else is going to work. You're picking up your newspaper and walking into your house, and everybody else is going the other way. Everybody else is just getting warmed up, and you're ready to hit the rack. Weird!

10-8

I was chasing a traffic-stop suspect on foot the other night when I suddenly realized three things. One, I had left my squad running in the middle of the street, with the door open. Two, there was another jerk in the car I had just stopped. And three, I wasn't going to have a heart attack over some jerk with no driver's license. So I pulled up after about a block, tucked in my ego, and slunk back to the squad. It all happened so fast that I didn't even have time to call out the stop or the chase. The suspect's car was gone, my squad was still there. I just got in and drove away like nothing ever happened.

10-8

Three things every cop really needs: common sense, caution, and worldliness. A cop who has been blessed with all three will be quite formidable. Unfortunately, I'm not one of those.

10-8

The greatest control a cop can exert over other people, be they witnesses, bystanders, or arrestees, is *mind control.* It's not done with guns or handcuffs or batons. A cop needs to communicate respect for other people's needs and desires, to demonstrate that our job is to work with citizens to achieve certain goals in certain situations. When I'm making an arrest, I use empathy with my arrestees. I try to understand what they're going through, and I let them know I'm trying to understand. I let them vent (to a point), if they feel the need. This usually works well for me. Of the 1,200 people or so whom I have personally arrested, I've had real problems with maybe three or four.

10-8

The other night on a midnight shift we had a smash-and-grab at a jewelry store in our downtown beat. I got sent over to do the evidence work. So I was busy taking pictures and glass samples and fingerprints when this dude with a video camera shows up. Which is kind of unusual because it's 4:00 in the morning. Next thing I know somebody tells me they saw me on TV. You never know. I will say that I would much rather be on TV talking about fingerprints than shown beating the crap out of some perp who deserves it anyway.

10-8

What's the difference between a rookie and a veteran cop? I could go on about that all day. I suppose the biggest difference is *attitude*. Rookies tend to be more idealistic, less forgiving, more by the book, more nervous. Veterans are far more pragmatic, more forgiving, and more self-confident. A cop who's been on awhile has the benefit of learning from his and others' mistakes, and thus has a better feel for what will work in any given situation. A rookie is still making those mistakes, trying to feel his or her way around. Rookies want and believe that they can go out and change the world. Veterans know that it just ain't possible. Not all rookies act like rookies, and some veterans still keep making the little mistakes that rookies make.

10-8

The worst call I ever heard dispatched over our areawide band came on a hazy, summer, Sunday morning. Two state troopers were killed, one right after the other, while answering a suspicious auto call. The place where it happened was far away, and normally the call would not have been broadcast in our area. But bad news travels quickly. All they had for leads was a vague vehicle description. When you hear a broadcast like that, it just leaves you numb.

10-8

Most jobs, when you go to work, you pretty much know what to expect. With our job, you can expect a few certain things to happen at certain times, but you really never know what could happen from one moment to the next.

10-8

Recently, while checking a building on the midnight shift, I found an open door that led to the parts warehouse at our local Chevy dealership. Imagine me being totally alone among thousands and thousands of Chevy auto parts. Of course, I drive a Ford!

10-8

A funny thing. Cops should really avoid politics like the plague, but we're stuck dealing with heavy-duty politicking on our jobs! Police departments have more of that going on internally than you could believe.

10-8

This is an example of a good suspect vehicle description: a late-model, light blue Chevy Corsica, four-door, with Illinois license plates XYZ 123, last seen going northbound on Main Street.

10-8

This is an example of a bad suspect vehicle description: a white car.

10-8

Another wonderful benefit of working midnights. You know all those weird little fevers your body goes through at night while it's trying to heal itself, when you're supposed to be asleep? Well, now you can experience those first-hand, wide awake, up close, and personal. Thank you. Not to mention the thing that happens to guys naturally at about 5:30 in the morning. Now that can be embarrassing.

10-8

A local charge is a slap on the hand. A state charge, look out! Higher bond, bigger fine, goes on your permanent record, and possible jail time. Whoa! How to get a local charge instead of the big one? *Cooperate* with the PD. Don't fight or lie about your previous record. Don't *have* a previous record. Maybe give up some decent information. Donate heavily to the local police benevolent fund. Just kidding on that last one.

10-8

I did a few room diagrams for some jewelry store burglaries we had. Then one of our arson investigators asked if I wanted to be the diagramer for the arson investigation squad. I was thinking about the heavy-duty overtime when I asked what happened to the last diagramer. "Oh, he drew something in the wrong place." One mistake. I took a pass.

10-8

A cop calls you at home and politely asks you to come down to the station for a little chat. You might as well come right out and ask him what the bond is, and bring it. It makes life so much easier. But don't get evasive, don't make excuses, and don't say you're going to come down and then not show up. Because then it'll be warrant time, baby. And we'll be pissed. And you'll get picked up, probably at just the wrong time and place. Like at your wedding or something.

10-8

One tough thing to do: tell someone you've known and respected for over ten years that you just arrested his son for DUI and driving with a revoked license. Not easy at all.

10-8

Don't expect me to get too excited about a barking-dog complaint. You know where the damned dog is, and you know who owns it. Get your butt over there and tell the owner to stifle it, okay? If that doesn't work, *then* call us.

10-8

The other night I went to a Taco Bell about a mile or so from my house for a little grub at about 10:00 at night. There were two armed security guys by the front door. What in the hell is this world coming to? I gotta run the gauntlet just to buy a damned burrito? Gimme a break!

10-8

When does it become really difficult to enforce a certain law, rule, or regulation? When the majority of the people affected by it believe that rule, law, or regulation to be wrong. Sounds a little simplified, but that's how some laws change.

10-8

What's the wackiest thing I ever charged anybody with? Unlawful use of horn. Somebody in the downtown beat leans on that car horn a little too long, I'm liable to lay it on them, ticketwise. So beware, all you compulsive honkers out there.

10-8

Almost every dissatisfied employee figures out some way to perpetrate a little sabotage in the old workplace, if you know what I mean. Cops do it. If we get pissed, we might quit arresting people or quit writing tickets. Or we might do the opposite and arrest everything that moves.

10-8

There are a few good reasons for a cop to get fired: too many brutality beefs; too many bribery complaints, coupled with some suspicious property acquisitions; too many complaints about the old pistola coming out of that holster; having sex with the wrong people; stealing; dealing dope. A cop should not be fired for: having too many complaints from scumbags; too many beefs with supervision and the administration; one beef from somebody well-connected; a "poor" attitude; refusing to take a polygraph test.

10-8

Do public safety officers have a greater obligation to be on the job than other workers? You betcha.

10-8

When you're on the shoulder of a highway, beware of that solid white line that separates the traffic lanes from where you are. Lots of times anything that ventures across it, or even near it, gets picked off at high speed. Call a friend, call a tow truck, put the hood up. But don't try any roadside repairs that involve getting near that line. Don't walk near that line, don't even ride a bicycle near that line. It's there for a very good reason. Death waits on the other side.

10-8

Occasionally while I'm making my rounds, I'll spot a fresh pile of garbage some goofy contractor has dumped behind some building or on some open piece of property. I've seen everything from a few rags and paint buckets to 10,000 pounds of chunk concrete sprout up overnight. I had a witness on the concrete caper. I telephoned the contractor, who'd piled it on a residential lot at the end of a secluded cul-de-sac. I told him to get it the hell out of there which, to his credit, he did. But a few days later, I spotted a suspiciously similar pile on another open lot at the other end of town. Careless, greedy, lazy people who choose to dump their garbage on the nearest open lot really make me angry. The least they could do is sneak it into a dumpster somewhere.

10-8

The other day a prominent doctor was shot and killed in his office in a town nearby. The suspect in the case was caught a few days later and gave a totally crackpot explanation for why he chose to kill a doctor. I wonder what goes on in the mind of a killer before and after he or she commits the act. I truly believe that if a person is determined and patient enough, if he or she wants to kill somebody, most likely that person will succeed. That's a very scary thought.

10-8

It really bugs me when some jerk gets pinched for some minor crime and then asks the judge for leniency because he or she is a so-called pillar of the community and a responsible person or a business leader. If anything, a person like that should get a *harsher* sentence, as an example. Really, two people with similar histories who have committed the same offense should get the same penalty. Unfortunately, equal justice will continue to be just a myth.

10-8

Today we had a holdup alarm call at one of our hotels, right at shift change. None of our units was near the area when the call came out and because the alarm was telephoned in by an outside alarm company, our own dispatchers wouldn't just pick up the phone and call down to the hotel to see if the alarm was a real one. So when another officer and I finally showed up, we both had to walk in without having any idea of what was going on inside the hotel. It turned out to be a false alarm, but I was so mad at the dispatchers for not calling that I called up the desk sergeant and chewed him out. Standard procedure for any holdup alarm activated at any business is to attempt to contact an employee by phone and get him or her to come out of the business if the alarm is false. If it's a genuine alarm, we find out right away from either the call or a call back to the department by employees. Cops have been killed taking holdup alarms too lightly, especially if there were several false alarms in a row at the same business. The next one could be the real thing.

10-8

Sometimes the administration eggheads institute new procedures that just plain backfire. A few years ago somebody in our department came up with the bright idea of issuing good-driver citations. If a motorist was driving in a particularly safe manner, we had the option to stop that driver and issue a safe-driving citation. As you can imagine, the local citizens got tired of that very quickly.

10-8

The other day, one of our dispatchers sent only one officer on this call: dead, bloated body lying in the driveway at such-and-such an address. But they'll send two officers plus a supervisor to a customer-management dispute. What's wrong with that picture?

10-8

It seems to me that most of the policy changes in our department come strictly from the top down, with very little input from the front-line patrol officers. We simply get a typewritten copy of the new departmental memo and maybe a fifteen-minute explanation.

10-8

Not too long ago I got sent on yet another raccoon-in-the-living-room call. Of course the couple in this nice house was completely helpless. But hey, they pay big taxes, so I grabbed the broom out of the home-owner's hand, opened the doors from the living room to the outside patio, and proceeded to bat that baby raccoon off the fireplace mantle and out the open doors. One minute, two minutes tops. Now that's service!

10-8

For many years we periodically got called about hunters firing shots in a large open field, bounded by woods, over on the north side of town. We'd zoom over there, but we never saw or caught anybody. Then last year some guy got caught shooting geese in the town north of us. The shooter lived right across the street from the open field. The conservation guys nailed this guy with a fine, confiscated his guns and his truck, and even searched his garage! It was slow in coming, but justice finally caught up with this jerk. Firing long-guns outdoors, within the city limits of a suburban town, is not too smart.

10-8

What is a career criminal? Well, you do three or four armed robberies or get busted selling drugs three times or get caught stealing cars a few times, you're on your way. Caught one time, maybe you should get a break. Three or four times same offense, shame on you.

10-8

Some people, especially drunks and some DUI defense attorneys, would like you to believe that a breath test or a blood and urine test administered as a result of a DUI arrest is unconstitutional, and thus is an improper search. Wrong, I say! These tests have nothing to do with the Constitution, and everything to do with licensing require-ments. Hey folks, a car can be a deadly weapon out there. You want to drive, you gotta practice, learn some rules, pass a test, get a work-ing car and insurance, and for God's sake you have to follow the rules. In my state, the very moment you get your greasy little hand on that driver's license, you are deemed to have already given consent to take a breath test, a blood or urine test, or any combination of tests when asked to do so by a police officer who has some probable cause. So you can forget the Constitution, you can forget your lawyer, and you can forget your Miranda rights. The hundreds of thousands of people who have died as a result of drunk drivers had the right to live. Everybody else who drives has the right to be safe from obnoxious drunks on our highways. So there!

10-8

I often wonder what our society would be like if everybody had more manners. If we just concentrated a little more on making other's lives a little easier, would crime go down? Treating people with some respect—hell, even acknowledging they exist—could go a long way toward preventing or even resolving certain situations before law enforcement intervention is needed.

10-8

Ah, RETIREMENT. That light at the end of the tunnel. I'm over half way to my twenty, but I won't be able to start collecting my pension until I'm fifty, which adds another year. I can't wait. I think I have enough interests to keep me busy to do whatever I want to do, all day, every day. That sounds pretty good to me! Right now, I never seem to have enough time to do all the things I want to do. And don't give me any of that time-management stuff. Just give me the rest of my life and a farm in Wisconsin. Then I'll be okay.

10-8

One cold, clammy, Sunday afternoon I got sent on an owl-being-harassed-by-a-crow call. Oh, come on! What the hell am I supposed to do on a call like that? Last time I checked, I didn't have wings, and I couldn't fly. But I rolled over there, anyway. Sure enough, when I got to the scene, I did see a large crow sitting on a high tree branch next to a small owl. The owl would fly to another tree and the crow would fly after it and land nearby. Pretty strange. Later I found out that crows hate owls, so I understood the dynamic a little better. Needless to say, I didn't do a damned thing. I just watched until they both flew out of sight.

10-8

Where to draw the line on phone taps, surveillance, and searches? I can't say exactly. The Constitution protects us from unreasonable searches. I personally believe that in order to search, two proofs must be met. Probable cause is one; reasonable, probable cause. The other is exigency. Will evidence or contraband be irrevocably lost or will society suffer if too much time is allowed to pass? Will a police officer's life be in danger? For the record, I believe a person's criminal history should figure greatly in the determination of probable cause. Sometimes the wrong people get rifled due to an error. People make mistakes, cops make mistakes, and informants can lie. So proper searches of the wrong people will occur. These people deserve some kind of compensation; not necessarily money, but something.

10-8

People who use violence to achieve political goals or to make a point or a statement about their beliefs have been with us for a long time. There are other ways to bring recognition to, and even resolve, certain issues. But these methods take more time, more cohesion, more planning, more intelligence, more creativity, more alternative thinking, more compassion, more openness....

10-8

Cops need longer vacations. *Everybody* needs longer vacations, like they have in Europe. We need more time away from the job to kick back, to ease that stress, to work out that tension. Seven weeks sounds good. That allows for about two weeks of raking grass or baking bread at the monastery. Nothing like a little dull, repetitive, mindless physical labor to help you work out your problems or appreciate not having any. No deadlines, no traffic, no TV, no radio, no crap. Just you, the rake, and the grass. Maybe if a lot of people tried this, we would be a lot more relaxed, less combative, and life in general would just be easier.

10-8

Watch out for terrorism. Being geographically isolated has helped us to a point. But a continuing high profile has brought us all kinds of attention we don't need. Americans have simply been too lucky for too long. Perhaps some of that evaporating defense money should be earmarked for anti-terrorism. The local cops aren't equipped to handle or prevent that stuff.

10-8

I truly lament the loss of the influence and wisdom of the extended family in our society. This socializing factor has suffered greatly from erosion as time goes by. Technology and its outgrowth, mobility, have effectively scattered American families to the point of no return. Even nuclear families are now feeling the onslaught. When they go down, how are our children going to be raised? By a computer? By one teacher? A book? A preacher? Without family members around, who will be the sounding board, the safety valve, the chaperon, the guide, the enforcer, the mentor, the example?

10-8

There's lots of talk lately about the need for more cops. We need more cops, it's said. They will be a deterrent. With more cops on the beat, crime must go down. I'm not so sure. There's been talk of an Explorer-type program, wherein qualified candidates can get some free college in exchange for a few years on the cop job. Skipping pension and a few other bennies for these short-timers would save some dough, and we'd have more coverage. Throwing more bodies out there isn't the final solution, though. You want to see a huge drop in crime? Legalize adult consensual crimes, such as gambling and prostitution. Save lives, save billions, ease jail overcrowding, reap big taxes, and apply the extra dough to devising real solutions to real crime problems.

10-8

A few years ago this guy got into a traffic altercation out on the highway with a couple of good ol' boys in a pickup truck. Big mistake. These two bears got out and proceeded to take it to the guy's car with a hammer and a hatchet! I thought it was kind of funny myself. Another time a sixty-five-year-old guy beat the crap out of a sixteen-year-old kid over a little traffic problem in the parking lot of one of our grocery stores. Be careful who you screw with out there. That could be Joe or Jane Maniac behind the wheel. If you get pissed, count to ten, talk it off, cuss, but don't mess with the unknown if you can avoid it.

10-8

Here's one for the "stupid local city ordinance" file. During the spring, summer, and fall, our fair city is virtually overrun with lawn-maintenance crews. Gas-powered leaf blowers have really come into vogue with these guys. They do a fantastic job on the leaves, but they're just too loud and obnoxious. Now we have a local ordinance banning leaf blowers...sort of. The push-'em-along-the-ground leaf blowers can be used all year long. But the backpack models are banned during the summer. We get people calling the PD about these things all the time now, and we actually have to roll on the dumb calls, punch incident cards, and even write tickets. Hey, I personally hate the damned things myself. All they do is eat up gas and make a tremendous racket. But let's get real. Just ban the suckers outright.

10-8

Let me reiterate: If we don't prove that we will back up our requests for compliance or cooperation with force time after time, then scumbags and even your ninety-year-old grandmother will simply tell us in no uncertain terms, "Up yours!" We can't afford to let criminals think they have the upper hand. We want criminals to fear us, fear what we can and will do to them. It may sound harsh and simplistic, but you try standing there figuring out how to handle some 300-pound maniac on drugs, and you will understand. Until we can prevent crimes by studying causation, that's the way it's gotta be. And sometimes, for one reason or another, excessive use of force will happen.

10-8

What is excessive? Well, how about using more force after compliance has already been gained and the situation is under some kind of control? How about using deadly force in a situation that does not demand its use? How about using force that is above the level needed to effect an arrest? Or going way, way beyond what has been set by departmental policy? Cops have a tremendous amount of discretion out there, and we know it. Like I said before, there's hundreds of thousands of cops out there. Some just don't know or have no control over their use of force. I'm not going to make any excuses for them. They get found out pretty quickly.

10-8

Calling all women, calling all women and some cross-dressers. Do you know that there is one thing about you, no matter what you look like or how old you are, that is always very attractive? It's your *purse*. It's a magnet. Two rules. First, don't keep too much in it. Second, never lose sight of that puppy. Believe me, you don't want some scumbag getting his paws on your driver's license, your credit cards, your checkbook, or worse, your house and car keys.

10-8

We have an anti-drug tactical unit operating in our area. The unit is separate from our department, but it borrows officers from local departments for about a year or so. These young guys and gals are the best. They go after it with a very serious can-do, kick-ass attitude. I'm sure their job must get really frustrating sometimes. But they must feel pretty good about themselves and what they are doing, putting drug dealers and users in jail and getting dope off the street. I've had the privilege of being in on capers with these fine officers, and their let's-run-with-it style never fails to amaze me. They're never exactly sure what they're going to be up against when a bust goes down. The danger level is significantly higher in this line of police work because of this. I tip my hat to these agents.

10-8

One time I had half an eye peeled for these two local marginal citizens who I knew were tooling around town with suspended driver's licenses. I didn't see hide nor hair of either one for months. Then I ended up popping them both on the same day. Not too bad for one eight-hour shift in a town of over 30,000.

10-8

Cops should probably be more into public relations. But we're so busy kicking ass and making people miserable that it's rather hard to do. Well, maybe we're not that busy. I regret that over the years of my career I didn't spend more time just stopping and talking to people. I know I feel good when I've answered a question or helped out with some little problem. Often just *listening* can do a lot. Our salaries are paid by the public. I suppose the least we can do is be responsive.

10-8

Thank you, all you greedy personal injury lawyers, for directly contributing to the over-litigious society we now have to wade through. Yes, there are true grievances that have to be redressed. But, hey, based on all the absolute crap I've seen and been through, the word frivolous doesn't even come close to describing a lot of the litigation jamming up our court system in this country. The frantic search for deep pockets is on. Hell, the frantic search for *any* pockets is on. Trolling around endlessly for little loopholes, picking over every little nit and tit, seems to be occupying the time of many of our nation's attorneys. The guys we trust to sort things out are the guys who are raping us. And believe me, it doesn't take much to find scapegoats, twist and turn and exaggerate the truth, and posture, and threaten, and red tape. I mentioned truth, well, you can replace it with money. And when people's jobs and lives and families are on the line, the lawyer has the gall to grab more than a third. A third of somebody's life for God's sake, for what? It sucks, it's greedy, and it's wrong. Huge bucks are luring these guys and gals out of nowhere. Everybody is getting sued. Paramedics, cops, nurses, doctors, even people with no money! Everybody is sweating liability out on the street, and we're all paying for it. Lost jobs, spiraling insurance rates, costs that are directly passed on to the consumers. And where does all this hard-earned money go? Into the pockets of fat and not so fat law firms so Bruce can get a new BMW. And that greed spreads. Now everybody is looking to sue somebody so they can have the money when they get sued! Or we're too busy looking over our own shoulders. One time I was rear-ended by a large truck operated by a contracting firm. They jerked around my insurance company, so I decided to call one of those injury lawyer firms. I had a sore neck, but I didn't need to call for an ambulance, I didn't rack up a huge medical bill and take time off from work, and I didn't wear that stupid neck collar that the attorney wanted me to wear. Well, the settlement was too long in coming, so I called the insurance company directly. To my dismay I discovered that my attorney was asking for too much. So I bought him off the case and settled it myself.

10-8

Pornography. Let me attempt to address this issue with my own feelings. We are sexual beings. To me this is beyond doubt. A lot of what we do and how we think is defined by our sexual orientation. Now I do believe that *child* pornography is a real crime. Children deserve their age of innocence. They shouldn't be preyed upon by greedy perverts. Adult porn is another subject. If it's discreet, not out of hand, and kept away from kids, it's not a problem with me. For some people, this is their only sexual outlet. Spice. Some people need more spice. And don't you ignorant zealots out there try to tell me or others how to live. I personally don't frequent porn shops. But I reserve the freedom, the right, to do so if I wish. Don't try to impose your narrow, strict, confining beliefs on others.

10-8

Why do people complain so much when cops hide while they're working traffic? I take great pains when I hide. It makes my job a lot easier. I know it's not "fair" to hide, but if you can see me you'll tighten up and follow all the rules. You won't drive like you usually do, taking risks, taking chances, and just generally ignoring traffic rules and regulations. So I hide. And to alleviate boredom, I'm rather inventive about it. I hide in driveways, around corners, up the street, down the street, down in gullies, in the shadows, in the sun, behind bushes, behind buildings, behind other cars and trucks, behind signs, behind fences, over hills, around the bend, in the snow, behind trees, under trees. I've got my spots all over town. One of my favorite hiding spots of all time was in the bay of an abandoned carwash that was situated very close to a busy intersection on our highway. I would tuck back in there all cozy at night like a moray eel, then lash out and pounce on unsuspecting motorists who swam past my den. I was so close to the highway that even at night I could read the liquor labels on the half pints the drivers were drinking! It ended when they tore down the carwash and put up a gas station.

10-8

Hey, parents! Some kids can get along just fine without you. They're independent, self-motivated, self-starters, they have outside interests, whatever. But some kids really need you around for that extra hug, that praise, that discipline, that heart-to-heart, that stern lecture, that encouragement. *Being there and being involved.* Not smothering, but being a *guide*. It can really make a difference with some kids.

10-8

Joe Civilian, the difference between my job and yours can be seen easily. Take a gander at the walls in the lobby of any police department. You are bound to come across at least one plaque with a picture and a badge commemorating a cop who was killed in the line of duty. We have one in ours. You got something like that in your lobby?

10-8

The other night I pulled this kid over for speeding. He immediately jumped out of his car, ran up to me, and showed me these two tickets. He had already been ticketed for speeding on two separate occasions that evening. I couldn't do him. He'd already been done twice.

10-8

Taking the law into your own hands can be very risky. When you do that, most of the time you are *breaking* the law. I believe in the law because it provides guidelines and order. Without it, might would simply make right. When you or I take the law into our own hands, we cross a line. Once a man whose daughter had been brutally violated by some scumbag shot said scumbag dead in the courthouse during the trial. I'm sure he felt that justice meted out by the law would not be near enough payment for what had been done to his daughter. So he took matters into his own hands to *guarantee* fair justice. He was arrested, tried, and jailed. I'm not saying you should never take the law into your own hands. I'm just letting you know what can happen if you do.

10-8

Blessed be the peacemakers, for they are few and far between. There are some people out there who just have the knack for defusing potentially dangerous situations or settling disputes before they get out of hand. We need more of these people.

10-8

Sometimes I'll be chasing the bad guys in this certain area at the southwest corner of our town, an area where I grew up. It just seems kind of funny.

10-8

What will mentioning another police officer's name get you on a traffic stop? Not too much, unless you're a relative. It also depends on the relationship between the cop who stopped you and the other officer. One of our veterans used to deflate this tactic by simply telling the motorist, "He and I just had an argument, and we're not getting along."

10-8

Many of the surrounding jurisdictions have computers in their squads. They can receive calls from dispatch and send back dispositions on the computer. The bad thing is, we can't hear or see those transmissions. So a lot of the time we never know what's going on in the towns around us. Unless they choose to tell us over the radio. Which they seem very reluctant to do, even if they could really use our help.

10-8

One thing I worry about that might happen to me sometime: I'm on a call and I'm away from my squad for awhile. I come back and the sucker is gone. Not good. Not good at all. Then what am I supposed to do? Whip out my portable radio and say I lost a squad? Don't laugh, that kind of thing happens more often than you think.

10-8

A young woman was sexually assaulted while sunning alone on a private stretch of beach. The victim allowed a strange man to approach her in an isolated area. I can't give the details, but she was very lucky this time. In another case, a fourteen-year-old gal was standing near a street corner when this guy drove by her twice and then started to walk up to her. She ran away. Can you see the difference between the two? Gals, keep your antennae up. Try not to get caught alone with a stranger.

10-8

Last night a Lexus and a Mercedes were stolen from private residential driveways in our town and a third vehicle was burglarized. The three cases were within a block of each other. It turns out that the owners of the Lexus and the Mercedes left the keys in the cars, so car burglars got a big bonus and decided to upgrade and become car thieves. They even got a third set of keys from a Suburban in the area, but had to leave it because the scumbags ran out of drivers. Folks, *don't ever* leave keys in your cars.

10-8

I see nothing wrong with broadcasting information across the CB radio about vehicles wanted in connection with crimes that have just occurred. It would certainly give us a lot more eyes and ears out there. And we need all the help we can get.

10-8

Great day! I got rear-ended by some gal driving a huge Toyota Land Cruiser. I was stopped in my squad at a stoplight. This poor gal pulled up behind me and stopped. Then she took her foot off the brake. The juggernaut rolled forward and popped me. Bent back her front bumper, too. Imagine this lady coming home and having her husband ask her how her day went. "Well, it was going okay until I hit the cop car."

10-8

Affirmative action in policing: lowering hiring standards in an attempt to deploy a police force in the field that more accurately reflects the demographic racial mix of a certain area or district. I like the idea of a proper mix. Cops who are from the area, of the area, and of the people in the area can't help but be more effective. But I don't like the idea of having to lower standards. I do like the idea of concentrating more on reaching and hiring the required number of minority candidates who meet or exceed the current, standard, accepted guidelines.

10-8

Today I was hawking a stop sign to try and get a ticket. I couldn't get a speeder because it rained all day and I don't like running radar in the rain. So I had my sign all staked out, sitting back far enough not to be seen but close enough to see behind the stop sign a couple of car lengths. I could tell that lately none of our guys had worked this sign because people were not showing it much respect. I heard a slight noise to my left and turned my head in that direction for just a second. That's when a red Taurus blasted through the sign so fast that all I saw was its rear end when I turned my head back. I hate when that happens.

10-8

Cops come in all flavors. Sweet, sour, bitter, strong, weak, saucy, bland, hot, heavy, light, et cetera.

10-8

One time I broke the left front turn-signal lens on my squad while trying to push some guy out of the snow in a parking lot. Good job!

10-8

You go out to your mailbox to get the mail. You pull out of your driveway to go to work. You're walking the dog. Lo and behold, there is a squad car, just sitting by the curb on your street where you've never seen one before. Hey, you pay taxes, why don't you just approach demurely and ask, "Is everything okay?" That's how you do it. If everything's okay, he'll tell you. If everything is not okay and he or she feels you should know, you'll be told. We do get annoyed when people ask us what we're doing, but there is nothing wrong with being concerned about what goes on in your neighborhood.

10-8

How's this for a series of fateful events? Cop (myself) sits by stop sign needing to write ticket. Cop observes woman driver blow stop sign. Cop pulls over woman and writes ticket. After piling a ration of shit on cop, woman drives away before cop can hand her the ticket. Cop races after said woman and stops her again to give her ticket. Cop gets hot call at high school and tries to make U-turn to get going in right direction. Squad with lousy turning radius does not make it on first try. So cop backs up and tries again. Squad still does not make it, glancing off curb and losing right front hubcap. Cop does not know this and races to call. Cop completes call at high school and gets called to police station, where motorist claims aforementioned hubcap struck his vehicle and caused damage. Cop goes to put hubcap back on squad. Cop gets hubcap back on squad. Cop sees air valve not protruding through hubcap properly and tries to adjust valve. Cop rips open right index finger (trigger finger) on said hubcap and spurts blood all over squad. Cop curses loudly, repeatedly, and drives to hospital emergency room, where cop gets four stitches and a Novocaine shot that puffs up finger like a sausage. Cop goes on light duty for a week. Cop recalls pleasantly in the ER that he does not need a tetanus shot, because he had one at same ER at same time last year when he got bit by a raccoon in left index finger and had to get fourteen shots, including six in said left finger. Cop is examining new stitches lovingly when cop sees old scar in same finger from where cop tried to pull a hubcap out of a snowbank when cop first came on job. Cop asks self what all this means. Sleeping Beauty gets it from the spindle, cop gets it from hubcaps. There is a message here somewhere. But I, for the life of me, can't see it.

10-8

You've heard me praise the safe-driving record of truckers. But I have to say that there are two things they do that really piss me off. One is to drive too fast in bad weather and fill every ditch with jackknifed semis. The other is jamming themselves under the viaducts in our area on a regular basis. Guys, don't you know how high a semitrailer is? Jesus, get the hell out and measure if you have to!

10-8

Injured again on the job. At least they let me work the dispatch desk for the few days I'll be out of commission. The bosses could make me use up some of my sick time or put me on workman's comp. I'm not very good at dispatching. I'm not up on all the new procedures and that computer crap. And I tend to punt too many of the calls that I answer on the phone. So I barely know what I'm doing, it's hectic, and it's a pain in the ass. But I do relish the change of pace. It gives me a break from the road and helps me understand what goes on in the communications room a little better.

10-8

Police departments where you call and get a recording: I hate that. When I call a cop-shop, I want to talk to a *person.* When I call any-where, I want to talk to a person for that matter. I don't care how con-venient it is or how much time or money it saves, I get annoyed when I'm dealing with a machine on the other end of the line. I think it's bad for public relations, too.

10-8

The other day one of our cops jumped out of her squad just a bit too quickly when she rolled up on a serious car accident. The squad door bounced back and smacked her right over the eye and knocked her backwards. Hey, shit like this happens. She wasn't hurt too bad.

10-8

Two things cops don't like. We don't like it when we're speeding along the highway (justifiably) and other people follow in our wake.

We don't think it's cute. No one should be allowed to speed but us. The other thing we dislike is when people driving with their heads up their you-know-whats cut us off. This is a pretty good way to get a cop's attention. I've arrested five to ten people who did that to me.

10-8

The other day a defense attorney was really reaming me on the witness stand over a DUI arrest. I mean this guy was really making me earn my pay. Unfortunately for him, he picked a tough case to try and wiggle on. I had his client speeding on a pace of 62 mph in a 55 mph, plus improper lane usage. Not only that, but his client had a suspended license and blew a .14 on the Breathalyzer. The judge wouldn't give me the speeder. He barely gave me the improper lane usage. The judge said he had sympathy for the guy! What the hell for? The guy was driving drunk and with a suspended license, for God's sake!

10-8

Today while I was working the desk, a scumbag I've arrested a few times came in the front lobby of the PD with his "family." That being his wife and what I presumed to be their unwed teenage daughter and her kid. I've had many, many contacts with these people—all negative. I can recall being overjoyed when the house they'd infested for so many years was finally torn down and they moved out of town. Drugs, drunkenness, thefts, assaults, domestic batteries, sexual assaults, and God knows what else; this guy had a lot of the bases covered. I was in plainclothes, so I don't think the guy recognized me. I think his wife did, though. When I looked at this guy, I knew I was staring ignorance right in the face. That's what cops really have to deal with all the time. In this country, a free education can be found and gained anywhere, by anybody. The only investment is time. There are no excuses, only choices. An education is a valuable thing, regardless of income or social standing. Once gained, nobody can take it away. To be ignorant is a choice. And because so many people choose it, it's probably the one thing we cops have to combat the most. We don't have much patience or sympathy for it.

10-8

The other day somebody posted a handmade sign on the road. It said: COP AHEAD. Obviously they got tired of all the speeders whizzing by and posted it so people would slow down. We thought it was pretty funny.

10-8

Today I stopped to have a Coke with a defense attorney who's a friend of mine. He told me straight out that he was taking a certain case of mine to trial. He even told me exactly what his main issue was with the arrest. I thought about it for awhile. Then I told him straight out that it was a good issue to take to trial. That wasn't easy for me to say, since this guy's client was a scumbag. But the truth is the truth.

10-8

So, you think you've been stopped by the cops for no reason. You know you didn't do anything wrong. The copper who stopped you walks up to your car sheepishly and mumbles something about a hit-and-run accident or a reckless driver and then slinks away. Please, don't make a big issue of it. That cop did have some reason for stopping you. He was probably just too embarrassed to tell you what it was. It's only a minor inconvenience for you. Be thankful that we're not trapped in a police state. Be thankful that you won't have to give up your boots or a bribe to be let go. Be thankful that you won't just disappear. You are a free person in a democratic society, you have rights, and you will be free to go on your merry way if this kind of stop should occur.

10-8

Things to do when you have a bad intersection in town where many bad accidents occur. First, lower the speed limits leading to that intersection. Second, increase the lighting. Then improve signage or traffic control devices. Attempt to simplify traffic flow in the intersection; computers are very good at this. And lastly, employ high-visibility traffic enforcement in the area. Don't just sit around and shake your head every time there's another bad accident at that intersection and then not do anything about it.

10-8

How strong should a cop be? Stronger than the average Joe. But a cop can make up for any fitness shortcoming by simply being more cunning than the average person.

10-8

Kudos to those rare individuals who somehow manage to break the cycle of their own continuing criminality. Somebody should talk to those people and find out *how* they did it. What turns these people around from scumbag to saint, I can't really say for sure. Maybe a single brain-shattering, eye-opening experience does it. Sometimes a mentor or a special support person does the trick. Or just a fortunate happenstance, like a job offer or a small inheritance pops up at just the right time. It's my belief that those people who do turn themselves around are made of sterner, stouter, smarter, and more sensitive stuff. Breaking out of a constant criminal-behavior pattern may be prompted by certain external events, but it's still got to come from inside. I just don't see prison as the type of environment where this type of turn-around can be fostered.

10-8

My shift commander, a lieutenant, told me this one the other day. One time, when he was just a rookie, he got sent on a call of "a naked woman on top of the garage howling at the moon." He thought it was some kind of joke, but he went to the call, anyway. Imagine his surprise when he arrived on the scene and had to call for a backup to help him handle a naked woman on top of the garage howling at the moon. I wish I'd been there to see that one.

10-8

Sending criminals to college. I know it sounds off the wall. But compare the average cost to house one inmate or the cost of one criminal on the loose in society to the average cost of a college education. I'm not saying this is the perfect answer. It's just a thought.

10-8

Try to get something changed on your evaluation that is dead wrong in our department, just try. It's harder than pulling teeth, I'm here to tell ya.

10-8

Not very long ago, a woman who was obviously quite intoxicated appeared in local court. She further confirmed everybody's diagnosis by telling the judge to "Fuck off." The judge told her essentially the same thing when he sent her directly to jail for contempt of court. The gal registered a .26 on the Breathalyzer, after being assisted from the courtroom.

10-8

Today I was sent on a call where a woman was running down the hall-way of an apartment building shouting, "She's dead, she's dead!" With a call like that, you never know what to expect. It turns out that this woman was way out there, beyond Pluto. She had to be strapped and shipped. It was sad. But at least nobody was dead!

10-8

Okay, you got a traffic ticket, you have to go to traffic court, and you're confused. Talk to somebody who's been there first. If you can't or you're still confused, show up early and talk to the bailiff, the court clerk, the prosecutor, even the cops. Doing this could help you a lot. But do this before court starts, or you won't get the inside on what is really going to happen.

10-8

Cops are great observers of the weather. That's because a lot of the time the weather affects what we do. Snowy and slushy: motor vehicle accidents. Rainy and stormy: power outages, false burglar alarms, working traffic posts when the lights go out, guarding downed power lines. Deep snow or very cold: stalled and stuck motorists. Heavy rains: motor vehicle accidents, flooding. Very hot: fights, stalled motorists. Extremely nice, mild, sunny weather on a weekend: many, many motor vehicle accidents. So we are constantly keeping an eye on the weather.

10-8

Eau de Squad Car. I'm sure many of you who have never had the experience wonder what the interior of a squad smells like. Well, take a couple of years of sweat, add a pinch of cigarette smoke, throw in a dash of farts, and season that mix with a little bouquet of french fry, and you'll have a pretty good idea.

10-8

The other day on the 3-11 shift, we had a serious traffic accident: small pickup truck versus large oak tree. The driver and passenger were badly injured. It was actually touch and go with the driver for awhile. Seat belts or a combination of seat belts and airbags could have really made a difference in this one.

10-8

There should be a felony charge for chronic bullshit complainers, okay? We've got some people in town who have absolutely nothing better to do with their lives than to pick up the phone and bitch about this piddly-shit thing or that diddly-squat thing. Of course we would like to reach right through the phone and strangle these people. But no, we've got to do the public relations thing and humor them instead.

10-8

On our department all the biggest, baddest, meanest guys get sent to self-defense schools. Meanwhile, the rest of us poor willowy types who need it the most don't get to go.

10-8

Not long ago, I changed lockers for one that was in a better spot. Somebody saw me taking stuff out of my old locker, and then I went on a long vacation. Rumors spread like wildfire that I had quit. Hey, guys, I've got too many responsibilities. I can't quit this cake job!

10-8

The other day a cop from a nearby major metropolitan area was arrested and charged with more than seventy felonies. Once again, the criminal behavior of one individual negates all the good work and brings down the reputation of an entire department. Cops are people.

We make mistakes, and we're not perfect. When we really mess up, it's big news.

10-8

Sometimes I like to write poetry. Here's one I kind of like:

> Motion for "no probable cause"
> The defense is grabbing at straws
> Abusing this neat little clause
> So the guilty go free with these laws.

10-8

How smart do you have to be to be a cop? I can tell you that I know some cops who are not rocket scientists by any means, but they are really, really good cops. I know some egghead cops, too. They can and do use their prodigious brains to make a contribution. An IQ test is by no means an adequate measure of how good a cop can be.

10-8

What causes car accidents? Not paying attention, poor traffic control, poor vision, poor signage, mechanical failures, sleepiness, speeding, drugged driving, drunk driving, poor driving skills, going too fast, bad weather conditions, poor road surface conditions, failure to drive defensively, bad manners, improper passing, improper lane usage, failure to yield, disobeying traffic controls, construction, failure to have vehicle under control, improper backing, opening a car door into traffic, ignorance, insanity, age, medical problems, panic, confusion, hurrying, going too slow, failure to signal a turn or lane change, just plain old stupid bad luck, two vehicles attempting to occupy the same space at the same time, jaywalking, driving the wrong way on a one-way street, fixed objects usually on the side of the road suddenly jumping out in the middle of the road, all of Mother Nature's creatures that try to cross the road, pretending your car is a plane or a boat, darkness, the sun, bright lights, dim lights, no lights, UFOs, foxy women, natural disasters, having a bad day, having a bad life, divorce, PMS, screaming kids, screaming adults....

10-8

The other day I got sent on a damage-to-city-property call. That is not good. It means paper for sure. Photos of the scene. And God forbid, an investigation. The reporting party, a gal who had already left the scene and driven to her home, related that she saw a red convertible with teenage males in it driving recklessly down this one street. Subsequently, this woman located damage to the parkway grass at a certain corner. So I rolled over there and took a gander. There was a muddy, large rut across the corner at this one intersection. To make matters worse, there was a plastic trim piece from the offending vehicle lying on the parkway in the rut. So now I'm looking at a property-damage hit-and-run accident with additional damage to city property (the grass). *Big* paper. So I do the right thing. I pick up the muddy, torn up sod and lay it back over the rut. I take the incriminating piece of plastic and throw it in a puddle nearby. I call in "no damage observed" and drive away. My hands were muddy, my shoes were caked, and my pants were soiled. But it was worth it to get out of all that paperwork for some minor rut in the grass.

10-8

You're cruising down the highway at night. Suddenly, inexplicably, traffic is jammed. You creep forward for what seems like forever and then you see it up ahead. The flashing lights, flares, squads, smashed cars, ambulances, tow trucks, fire engines, and cops. Right away you know there's been a serious accident and people are hurt. You know that we're out there trying to put the pieces together. So please, do everyone a favor. Pray for the people involved in the accident. Pray for our safety. Thank God it wasn't you. Take your peek. And then drive on.

10-8

I wrote this woman a speeding ticket today on day shift. She was going 42 in a 25, and she gave me the old "sick kid" story. The kid didn't look so sick to me, so I proceeded to write her the ticket. Then she gives me the usual ration of shit, escalating into to calling me "nasty" and using the F-word. Not very ladylike, especially in front of her kid.

I gave her the ticket, and then told my shift commander the story in case she called up to beef me. Folks, don't beef cops just because they gave you a ticket. You got a beef about getting a ticket, take it to court and fight it there. Don't start making things up, like how rude the cop was, or that he or she was wrong. Supervisors have heard just about every excuse there is and will not take a ticket back just because you say the cop was rude. And believe me, cops have long memories for people who try that kind of crap.

10-8

The revenge factor looms large when you're a cop. You see, cops have access to more power and more resources than ordinary citizens. The temptation to abuse those powers and exploit those resources in order to strike back at some jackass who has made one's life miserable in some way is at times very hard to resist. The possibilities are endless. Traffic stops, setups, arrests, telephone harassment, assaults, criminal damage to property, et cetera. Just thinking about exacting revenge in those ways can give even the most upright cop the shivers. Most of us, of course, take revenge *only* in our imaginations. But sometimes I think about a worst-case scenario. What if somebody was too insistent and pushed me too far? I'm no saint. I have my limits. I always try to rise above the hate, to let it roll off my shoulders. I try not to think about what might happen if someday I can't do that.

10-8

Sunday mornings. Domestic violence time. The alcohol from the regular Saturday night binge is still on board. So we get the calls, and we roll. We have to look at the split lips, the black eyes, the bruises. We have to hear the stories of continual and unabated physical and mental abuse. And we get blamed a lot of the time for not doing our jobs, even though we've arrested the perp several times before and the victim always drops the charges and always forgives and welcomes the slick-talking, breadwinning, security-providing scumbag back into her life, only to be abused again. Another sick cycle completed. Our blood boils because we know we are not to blame, and we'd rather put an end to this crap right now by beating the living shit out of the abuser and then locking him (or her) up for about a decade or two. But we can't do that, even though we want to. The power to break the cycle of abuse is in the mind of the *abused person*. If you're on the wrong end of an abusive relationship, it's up to you and your support system to make the decision to break yourself out. Separation and intense counseling, or the road. I know you don't think it's that simple. But think about it the next time he or she abuses you. And there will be a next time.

10-8

Motorists who wave guns around at other motorists have to be classified as some of the stupidest people on earth. You flash a pistol at somebody, do you really think they're just going to cower and go away? Not! They're gonna call the cops, and the cops are gonna pull you over in your stupid little car and take your stupid little gun and throw your stupid little self in jail so fast your head will spin.

10-8

Having to get out of bed at night and go to work when the weather stinks is not one of my favorite things. When I hear the wind howling out there, I just want to stay in bed and pull up the covers. Instead, I have to get up, take a shower, shave, get dressed, and creep into work in the dark of night in the middle of some storm while everybody else gets to stay home in bed. I hate that.

10-8

First night back on midnights, I got a stray-dog call right off the bat. Somebody was holding the dog, so I couldn't punt the call. The stray turned out to be this really nice, male Husky-German Shepherd mix. He was only a pup, but he was so quiet and well-behaved I wished I could've kept him. I was glad to know that the owner came and picked him up from the pound a few days later.

10-8

Recently a friend of mine got into some real trouble, and by fate I happened to be involved in this guy's arrest. He had never been arrested before, but what he did this one time was pretty serious. I made a few phone calls, pulled a few strings, and then walked him though his court appearance. He and his attorney entered and received a very good plea bargain in the case, and the guy didn't have to go to jail. After court, we went to the clerk's office, and after that we walked over to the adult supervision offices. This experience, a first for me, gave me a pretty good feel for what it's like to be charged with a crime. It was a real eye-opener, allowing me to see things from the other side for a change.

10-8

In our municipality, the city manager is the direct boss over the police. It's very important to us that the city manager be pro-police. When we get some guy who is on some kind of political soapbox for himself or gets really hung up on the "seven principals of sound management" stuff, well, we know we're in for it then. Getting any kind of cooperation or trust from guys like that is like pulling teeth. We don't need the next president of the United States, and we don't need a managerial Einstein. We just want somebody who is reasonable and who understands what our job is all about.

10-8

I've gotten real tired of hearing about situations like Rodney King. Let's hear instead about all the damage a guy like Rodney King does to our society before we start calling him a hero, okay?

10-8

Very few things on this job can compare to the feeling of satisfaction I get when reuniting missing juveniles with their concerned parents. In this day and age, even a brief unexplained absence can be cause for alarm. I understand this because I have kids of my own. Whenever I get a missing juvenile case, I drop everything and really throw myself into it. I'm a human whirlwind, running around checking leads, making phone calls, talking to other people, getting in contact with other police departments, et cetera. Telephone networking involving friends of the missing juvenile is for me the most successful way to get a line on the missing kid. Nine times out of ten, I can close out a missing juvenile case in less than four hours. Some kids come home on their own. Others finally call to check in. But most are just hanging out with friends. Then there are the other cases, the ones cops dread the most. The hours roll by with no leads. The hours turn into days. Possibilities run out. Worries escalate. Since I've been on my department, we've never really had the true, endangered abduction of a juvenile by a stranger. But I always think about the time when I'll get a missing juvenile case and I won't be able to find the victim. I really don't want to be the one who one day must go to the door without the child, with sad face and broken voice and the worst tidings any parent would ever want to hear.

10-8

The other night on the midnight shift was "triangle night." As anybody knows, three's a real crowd in the marriage game. Especially when hubby finds out about Mister Three. One guy in our town found out that another guy was giving his wife drugs in addition to helping make him a cuckold. So the wronged husband did the macho thing. He went over to Mister Three's house and proceeded to kick ass on the scumbag. Somebody else called on the phone in the middle of the fracas, and the husband answered it, giving Mister Three a chance at living. Which he took, by jumping right through a closed window and bolting the scene. Hubby, who was drunk, drove home and kicked butt on the old lady. We got three calls in a row. A fight at one house, an injured guy running around outside another house, and a domestic battery back at home. Triangle number two, which went down soon after, was even better. Wife goes out once with single guy and is nice enough to tell hubby about same. Hubby calls this Mister Three and says, "Hey, let's be adult about this and why don't the three of us get together for some drinks and discuss this." So it happens. After a few drinks, the hanky-panky is okay with hubby. But after lots of drinks, wife wants to go home with Mister Three, and suddenly it's not okay. Big husband chases little guy around parking lot, falls on face on rough concrete and needs thirty stitches. Justice.

10-8

Did I mention my support system? By that, I mean our dispatchers, records personnel, our janitor Hank, our auto mechanic Cosmos, our equipment supervisor Terrance, our crime lab people, and our branch court clerks. Without their faithful service, none of what I do out on the street would have any significance, any impact. Having good, dependable people in these positions is almost as important as having good cops on the job. We all operate as a team, even though we don't feel like it all the time.

10-8

Hectic, that's the word for it. It seems to me that as more time goes by, more people in our society are in more of a hurry, are generally more annoyed, and are always more pressured. I truly hope we all, and I'm including myself here, will consciously slow down the pace and think of others instead of just ourselves all the time.

10-8

This guy, Bob, who lives in our town is such a habitual barhopper that he's become probable cause for me. I've arrested him twice for drunk driving, so he has no driver's license and he doesn't drive. But every time I see him as a passenger in some beater car driving around town after the bars close, I automatically know that he and everyone else in that car, including the driver, will be drunk. So I take extra care to put a traffic stop on any car I see him in. Four or five times I've arrested a drunk driver when Bob has been a passenger. You'd think the word would get around and that no one would drive him home. But they still do. Which is okay with me. I always make sure to say, "Hi, Bob," right before I arrest his designated chauffeur for the evening.

10-8

Our uniform pants are 20% cotton and 80% polyester. When in the world are they going to come up with a durable, washable, comfortable uniform fabric that breathes, looks good, doesn't melt, and doesn't give your legs a rash?

10-8

The other night we got a call about a power line down across the road in a residential district on the east side of town. The fire department rolled up on the scene just as a homeowner was about to kick the downed line with his foot. "Hey, you, Buddy! You might not want to be doing that!" a fireman shouted. The upshot is that the fire engine took up a protective position on one side of the line and I drove around the block and blocked the other side with my squad. Looking across that line lying in the roadway in the gently falling rain put me in a contemplative mood. I thought about how cops and firemen have a common purpose, like tonight. Protecting people and property. But cops are cops, and firemen are firemen. And although most of what we do is for the same reason, how we go about doing our jobs is very different. After about half an hour the power company showed up. The engine went on its way, and I went mine. And once again, the world was made a little safer because we *all* did our jobs.

10-8

Several times I've had other cops testify against me in DUI trials. From the circumstances surrounding their testimony and the testimony itself, it's quite obvious they were lying, either because they were getting paid to do so or because they were doing their buddies a favor. I don't appreciate that crap. Not one bit.

10-8

Recently I attended a one-day seminar on domestic violence. A counselor from a local domestic violence court was very blunt about the success of rehabilitating offenders. She said counseling doesn't stop batterers. Jail time and fines from arrests don't stop them from continuing to batter. Court orders don't work, either. The only positive result of all these so-called remedies is that when the victim sees that none of that stuff works, the light bulb goes on and she does what she should have done much earlier to break the vicious cycle. *She leaves the scumbag.*

10-8

Small businesses, keep a hawkeye on that cash register, because there's a small, very determined group of people who don't work for you who are watching your cash drawer, too. They're called Till Tappers, and their life's work consists of getting their grubby little hands into your till and absconding with your hard-earned, untraceable cash. Till Tappers work alone, in pairs, and in groups. Their MO is simply to enter your store, divert your attention somehow, and attack your cash register. Leaving that drawer open all the time or unattended all the time is just fine with them. It makes their job easier. Don't leave too much cash in that drawer and guard that thing like your business depended on it.

10-8

Just about every PD has one or more officers who are more prone than others to having motor-vehicle accidents with the squad cars. You'll have guys with eighteen or twenty years on who have never been hit and who have never hit anything. And you'll have rookies who will have maybe eight or nine accidents in their first year or two on the job. My nickname was "Crash" for awhile.

10-8

One time one of our coppers was seriously injured while checking around a house on yet another bogus burglar alarm. I'm waiting for that to happen to me. Actually, I'm really waiting for some idiot homeowner to take a shot at me through the blinds while I'm checking the perimeter of his house on an alarm.

10-8

There's no feeling like the adrenaline-exhilarated panic you get while rushing in on a drug bust after a stake-out.

10-8

Very near the end of the long and arduous hiring process that culminated in me becoming a cop, the city doctor tried to bounce me off the final list because of some very minor thing about my back. I suppose he thought he was just doing his job, but I went ballistic after he called me at home on a Sunday to give me the news. It'd been a long haul and I really needed the job, and I didn't need to hear that crap. My own doctor came through for me, and after seeing a specialist I was finally hired. Ten years later I'm still going strong. My latest fitness evaluation was my best so far. Did I mention that I wrote the city doctor's daughter a ticket for speeding in a school zone a few years after I was on?

10-8

"Alleged" offenders paying big bucks to their living victims in order to avoid going to jail. I like the idea of victim compensation. But I'd hate to think that anyone with enough dough could buy out of some very serious criminal charges.

10-8

Items hanging on the inside of my locker door at work: a calendar, a high school ring I took off a drug dealer (it wasn't his), current subpoenas for court cases, notes on followups and cases, and one very special photo of a very special person. There is also a photo of the guy who had my locker before me who retired after twenty-five years of service.

10-8

We recently had to work through the worst cold spell on record where the outside temps reached down to 70° below zero with the windchill. It was brutal. My face, when exposed to the elements, froze in about thirty seconds. I have an old car and no garage to keep it in. I was running that thing every five hours around the clock for days and days. I got really tired of waking up at 4:00 in the morning just to go out and start my stupid car. But it ran. It ran because I needed it to.

10-8

One guy on our department has a knack for making some fabulous pinches by just being in the right place at the right time. He unleashes this awesome talent about once a year. One time there was this armed robbery at a gas station in our town. His shift was shorthanded, so he didn't get to the area of the call until some time had passed. He decided to respond with lights and siren anyway. On his way to the call, the bad guy just happened to pull out from a side street, right in front of our man. Just by chance. The perp thought the gig was up, pulled over to the side of the road, and got out of the car with his hands up! Another time, these three idiots were robbing a storage trailer in the parking lot of a hardware store, and they got spotted. An areawide broadcast was put out with the description of the vehicle and the offenders. The town where the theft went down was many miles away. So who spots the vehicle, puts a stop on it, and recovers about $60,000 worth of stolen property? Our magic man.

10-8

Recently we had this vehicle accident out on the highway where a drunk driver struck the median and flipped his car, causing a serious injury to another motorist and a minor injury to himself. A records check through the SOS (Secretary of State) revealed that the offender had a revoked driver's license. This excuse for a human being had five separate convictions for drunk driving on his record in three months!

10-8

While I was on foot patrol in our business district, I got a radio call about three suspicious subjects milling around a car in a parking lot nearby. So I strolled over to check out the situation and caught three drug addicts who'd just stolen hundreds of dollars worth of merchandise from a nearby store. They would have gotten clean away, but their car wouldn't start! Justice!

10-8

One night this poor gal called the PD and reported that a man in a blue-and-green plaid shirt was looking in her living room window. Which was no big deal because stuff like that happens all the time. Only the complainant lived in apartment 413. You know—on the fourth floor of a building that has no balconies.

10-8

Another time this woman drove her car right through the glass doors of our local hospital emergency room. She pulled right up to the astonished nurse working the admissions desk and told her that she needed help because she was being chased by Martians who were talking to her through her garage-door opener. Talk about drive-up service!

10-8

Last night I wrote one motorist eight tickets. What kind of tickets would that be, you might ask? How about driving under the influence of alcohol, driving with a blood-alcohol content above .10, speeding, failure to signal lane changes, operating a motor vehicle with suspended registration plates, open transport of an alcoholic beverage, driving with a revoked license, and a local charge for possession of marijuana. Eight tickets may seem a little excessive, but, hey, I could have written him ten. I gave him a break on no insurance and improper use of vehicle registration, sweet guy that I am.

10-8

Studies show that a distressingly large number of our convicts were born to teenage mothers. You want to reduce crime, then reduce teenage pregnancies. And don't you anti-abortion advocates get bent out of shape. There are other ways to reduce teenage pregnancies.

10-8

I wonder if it's true about the average victim of domestic violence leaving the abuser seven times before finally getting the message and staying away for good. That sounds about right to me. My neighbor is up to number six, I think.

10-8

The strangest thing I've ever had to photograph on an evidence technician photography assignment was an ear. One sunny Sunday afternoon these two guys got into a fight in the backyard of this house. During the scuffle, one bit the ear off the other. I was dispatched to the scene to photograph the ear, which I did. I then had to pick it up and take it to the hospital, where it was re-attached to its grateful owner. It was pretty gross, but you have to do what you have to do.

10-8

The other day I got my first electrician call. I was handily dispatched to this apartment building in our business district in the middle of the night to try to get this poor gal's electricity back on. Initially, I was not too thrilled and mentioned something about not having my insulated rubber gloves with me. But when you're sent, you gotta go. So I rolled over there, assessed the situation, told the gal to turn off about eight of her appliances, went down to the basement, and turned the massively overloaded but now not so loaded circuit breaker from OFF to ON, and presto! Wait until she gets my bill.

10-8

Early one Christmas morning I found myself on the way over to this real jackass local citizen's house. I was carrying two five-gallon buckets of horse-shit that I was going to leave in this jerk's driveway as a special Christmas greeting. But when I got there, the guy's house was all lit up with Christmas lights. There was no way I was going to pimp a guy on Christmas day when he had a great exterior light display. I just threw the buckets in a dumpster. It did take about three hours of driving around with the back windows open before the smell dissipated from my squad.

10-8

One time we had this rollover motor-vehicle accident that happened late at night in a dark, more rural part of town. The whole affair went unwitnessed, and six unlicensed, uninsured, illegal, and unsober former occupants fled the scene and somehow managed to limp back to the barn. The seventh occupant was nowhere to be found the next morning when the others arose with sore necks, backs, and heads and were sober enough to take a body count. Their unlucky friend, to their horror, was ultimately discovered flattened like a pancake underneath their overturned vehicle.

10-8

Another time, paramedics were very busy extricating, treating, and packaging for transport several seriously injured occupants of an accordioned station wagon. They were just getting ready to leave when they thought they heard muffled sounds coming from the wreck. The sounds emanated from the frantic lips of yet another casualty, a fella who'd been perfectly sandwiched between the front and back seats. Expecting to discover grievous injury, the paramedics worked frantically to pry their patient from the car. They were overjoyed when this last passenger was finally freed and needed only treatment for a broken ankle.

10-8

How about mandating lower levels of alcohol in wines and beer? That way people could still get their kicks without the massive alcohol injection. Just a thought.

10-8

The other day I had this guy in custody at the PD for some traffic charges. I was getting ready to process my mope when a rookie happened to stroll behind this guy. He started making faces and pointing to the back of my mope's head. I thought I saw him silently mouth the word bugs, so I stood up and walked around behind the dude. Sure enough, I saw two large brown *bugs* crawl out of the guy's hair onto the back of his baseball hat. And the guy didn't look that scummy, either! I just prayed that those little suckers couldn't jump, processed the guy, and got him the hell outta there!

10-8

Deliberate acts of pyromania do occur at the police station now and again. Unhappy detainees, when left to their own devices in the company of a book of matches, sometimes put two and two together and do something that makes us pretty miserable. It doesn't help their cause too much, either. The last time it happened, our Breathalyzer got smoked and had to be shipped for repairs. Gee, thanks.

10-8

Another great ruling by a judge. I see a guy driving with his eyes shut. He's straddling the center line of two southbound lanes of traffic in front of me for more than 100 feet. But the judge says I have no probable cause to pull the guy over because he's not doing anything wrong. Give me a break, would ya?

10-8

One of our coppers was rolling harmlessly around the north end of our business district on a midnight shift. He eyes these two idiots fooling around with two cars pulled over to the curb and stops to investigate. End result: recovery of two very freshly stolen Porsches worth about fifty grand apiece, and two suspects in custody. These perps very efficiently purloined two swell cars, but then decided to stop only two blocks away to put license plates on them. Thank you.

10-8

Talk about robbing the bank next to the donut shop. We have this little shop in town where cops get a really good deal on deli sandwiches. So we hang around the place like flies on you-know-what. And people still try to shoplift sandwiches while we're in there in full uniform shooting the bull or waiting for our Dagwoods to be made. And if we're not there and the store clerk sees something hinky go down, all he or she has to do is step outside the front door and wave, because sure as shootin' one of us is about to pull into the parking lot. It sounds silly, but aside from the PD itself, this place is by far the most well-guarded in town!

10-8

If you really think of it, sex, drugs, and alcohol are the only forms of excitement our young people go for these days. Where on earth do they learn that behavior?

10-8

Very recently I arrested this scumbag for DUI. He was legally drunk (a .11), had a revoked driver's license for DUI, had multitudinous open beers in his motor vehicle at the time of his arrest, had been arrested for DUI twice before in the last five years, and had a broken leg at the time of the arrest due to a fall down some stairs, probably when he was drunk. And despite all that, he insisted that he wasn't a drunk. I'd sure as hell like to know what this guy uses for his criteria in determining what a "drunk" is!

10-8

I just saw a wonderful movie about a true story wherein, through his own daring, bravado, and finally compassion, one man saves the lives of about a thousand people. While not trying to sound too boastful, in my own case I can only hope that out of all the arrests I've made up to this writing, that I will have saved at least one or two or maybe more lives outright through my enthusiasm and persistence through adversity in pursuing drunk drivers. I may never push a child out of the way of a speeding train. I may never save an innocent person from the ravages of a madman during my career. But when I retire, I will be able to say, beyond a doubt, that I did save lives and that I did prevent harm to innocent people in this one small way. That will be my greatest contribution as a law enforcement officer.

10-8

Many times I've been dispatched to calls involving teenage girls with psychological problems, either mild and temporary or more permanent and severe. In my experience, the single most contributory factor to their problems, outside of abuse, is these girls' total lack of respect for their mothers. A mother is an important role model. If young girls see their mothers take a fall either from drug or alcohol addiction, from a bad divorce, or from their own mental problems, they can be affected adversely to a tremendous degree. A lot of the girls are smart enough and sensitive enough to see what the hell is going on with Mom, and they lose their own chance to learn and build self-respect and self-confidence.

10-8

Every morning right at the beginning of the domestic battery court call, several "lucky" men are called up to the bench and their cases are dismissed because their significant others have dropped the charges and will not testify. I don't like to see that. I don't like to see their arrogant, self-righteous, I-didn't-do-anything-wrong attitudes. Well, all you "lucky" guys, your little free rides will soon be over. The courts and the criminal justice system are finally seeing the light. Soon we will be able to charge abusers and prosecute abusers and punish abusers *without* the testimony of the victims.

10-8

Many times I'll come home after work and notice that I still have some fingerprint ink on my hands. This serves as a small but insistent reminder that I've busted somebody that day. It's not always a positive thing with me. A lot of times it just tells me what a lousy job I have.

10-8

What do you do if you take a peek in your rearview mirror and then get the distinct feeling that someone is following you? Do not pull over and try to have a little chat. Try to drive immediately to the nearest police station or to a very public place and then call the police. And try to get the license plate number of the other car. It could just be a friend, or somebody who has mistaken you for someone else, or somebody you got in a traffic thing with and flipped off and who just wants to yell at you, or some pervert who likes how you look and wants only to play around with you. Or it could be somebody who is totally loony tunes and wants to do you major harm. Don't give that person the opportunity.

10-8

One time this supervisor got a little over-confident and made a rash vow: If this one case turned out a certain way, he would climb the flag pole in front of the PD, naked. Well, against some pretty heavy odds the case did take that twist and, to his credit, the sergeant did make that ascent. He did it at night, though.

10-8

It's taken me years, but I've finally figured out exactly what deputy chiefs are for. Their main purpose on the job is to pull rookies aside in the hallways at the PD and say, "I heard you did such-and-such. Don't do that anymore." I've benefitted from at least two or maybe three of those little meetings.

10-8

I wrote yet another lucky motorist eight tickets the other night. I consider it part of my continuing education of drunk drivers.

10-8

Cops have to make a lot of decisions during the course of a shift. Some are minor, and some can have a major impact on life as we know it. When I was in college, I went to a concert in a basketball arena and saw what was probably one of the dumbest decisions ever made by a cop. This was in the '70s, and it was a rock concert. This young cop who's working security decides he's gonna bust this dude for pot. Only the dude is standing right smack dab in the center of about 5,000 other dudes and dudettes who at the time were very sympathetic to pot use and very, very unsympathetic to right-wing, pig-type, rights-crushing cops. I remember distinctly seeing this poor copper enter the mob at one corner. A whole lot of fists and arms went flying around the center of the crowd. The last thing I saw was this very lucky cop squirting out of the other side of this fired-up bunch, minus hat, badge, probably gun, and a few other things, like dignity.

10-8

Here's another one for the "that's eerie" department. One night I had to handle a car accident involving an eighteen-year-old white female who lost control of her T-Bird on a side street and flew off the road. Two nights later I got another accident involving another eighteen-year-old female white driver in a T-Bird from the same year who also drove off the road. Neither gal was injured seriously. The first T-Bird was white and the second one was black, and I remember thinking to myself, "What does this mean?"

10-8

So I'm working the midnight shift. For the last three nights we've had to dedicate one street officer from our shift to the task of watching some scumbag who got in a wreck in our town while in a stolen car and ended up in the hospital. That makes me irate. We have to work with less coverage out there on the road because some pea-brain administrator has yet to figure out that the most important function of the police department is patrol.

10-8

Community Policing. Sounds good to me. Cops reaching out, being seen, felt, and heard. That's the key.

10-8

Reasonableness. A good term. The standard against which a lot of what we do is measured. The exact definition of Reasonableness may be hard to pin down. But it's a start.

10-8

Let us never forget the thousands of survivors of those who have fallen in the constant battle against crime and ignorance. The husbands, the wives, the children, the relatives, friends, and co-workers whose lives were shattered and who are left in a daze, picking up the pieces, wondering how such a horrible thing could happen and where do we go from here. Probably the greatest thing you could do for us is to remember all our heroes, and what they stood for.

10-8

When I get a stolen-auto report where said auto gets yanked from the reporting person's house or work, the first thing I do is ask to see the payment book. Many times it turns out that the "stolen" car has really been repossessed due to late payments.

10-8

Summertime. Two big things I can count on. For sure my left forearm is going to get darker than my right. And we are going to be busy, real busy. Because when it gets really hot, please just quadruple the number of calls, okay?

10-8

Cops and Sex. Yup, these two items butt heads every once in awhile. Cops go on lots of calls, rubbing up against members of the opposite sex many times under stressful conditions. It's extremely likely that at some point in some situations either the cop would like to have sex, or the victim or other party would like to have sex, or they both would like to have sex. I am neither condoning it, nor am I passing judgment. I'm just saying that it happens with this job.

10-8

Here's an indicator about how stressful this job can be. A few years back, I was having one of those really bad days. It was mid-winter and the weather (as usual) was absolutely lousy. Lots of cold and lots of snow, translating directly into me having to push about six or seven cars out of snowbanks that day. Well, I get a little break and decide to roll over to the hospital ER and make a pitstop. While in the hospital parking lot, I push yet another auto out of yet another snowbank. I go into the ER, make one aggravating phone call, and after that just by chance I ask a nurse I know if she has time to take my blood pressure. Okay, she does—175/125! Next thing I know, I'm lying in Bay 6 with part of my uniform off and one of those goofy hospital gowns on. I managed to calm down to 140/90 in about twenty minutes. There was one positive thing that came out of all this. The ER doc gave me a scrip for a stress test, which I took three weeks later. I checked out okay, but I was glad to have had the test.

10-8

People are driving faster all the time. Believe me, I'm out there in the street every day in a good position to see it, feel it, hear it (and ticket it). By my estimation, we're experiencing an increase of a little less than one-half a mile per hour a year. That doesn't sound like much, but after ten years, that's an average increase of 5 mph. Not good, not good. It's probably a me-first/stressed out kind of thing.

10-8

Remember, just because your car has air bags doesn't mean you should drive without your lap/shoulder belt secured. Air bags are designed to work in *conjunction* with seat belts, okay?

10-8

Critical Incident Stress Debriefing. Remember those words. Somethines cops see things, bad things, that they cannot forget. They're involved in shoot-outs. They sometimes see people commit suicide (as one of our coppers did recently). Sometimes it's a bad accident or a terrible child-abuse case. Folks, once observed, these things don't just go away without some kind of help. They get in there and fester, sometimes taking only hours, sometimes years, to surface. Critical Incident Stress Debriefing can help short-circuit this cycle and may end up saving some poor copper's life. Or anyone else's for that matter, who's been subjected to these kinds of things.

10-8

Working on a movie production is a great extra job for a cop. You don't have to work too hard, the food at the canteen is usually fabulous, and you get to see some real movie stars up close and how movies are made. The hours are a bit unusual, however, and they certainly are long. One movie I worked on filmed from 4:00 in the afternoon to 4:00 in the morning. One night at about 2:00 in the morning, this yuppie couple drove right onto the set in their little Mazda, right past where we were standing. Thank God they were taking a break in the shooting! We strolled up to this guy and his girlfriend and nicely asked him what the hell he thought he was doing. He said he was driving up from the city and got lost. We said, "In case you haven't noticed, this is a movie set, so could you please get lost somewhere else?"

10-8

The people in an "exclusive" town near us were always calling their PD in a panic about this or that black person they'd seen in their neighborhood. The "suspect" was maybe just passing through, minding his own business, or trying to sell magazines subscriptions. This particular PD hired a black cop. Nice guy. Did his job. Reflecting the kind of warped sense of humor cops have, the PD started sending him out whenever they got one of those vague calls. I can see it now. Resident dials PD, mumbles something about a suspicious black man in the area, black cop rolls on the call, walks up to the front door, and says to redfaced resident, "Now just what was that man doing wrong, anyhow?" "I, er, well, I, uh...." One time a gal called that PD to report a stolen squad car with a black man at the wheel. What she'd seen was this black cop driving around on patrol. Gimme a break!

10-8

Cops are always checking out driver's licenses for staple holes. Those tiny relics from the past can serve as an unofficial driving record. More holes, more tickets have been given previously. No holes, maybe a clean driving record. Staple holes in the *face* of the photo on the license, bad attitude.

10-8

Okay, okay, you screwed up and got arrested for some minor bullshit. Nobody likes to get busted, we know that. So we do give you a litle griping leeway. You can tell us we were wrong to arrest you. You can tell us it wasn't your fault. You can say we're unfair. You can even call us assholes. We can take that; we're used to it. You can even stretch it and insult our mothers or our wives. But don't, and I mean don't ever, *ever* say something like "If I see you out of uniform I'm gonna kick your ass!" You don't know it, but you just stepped into the twlight zone. We hear that, and it's already too late for you, pal. Not only does the ticket book warm up (again), but you get an added bonus—immediate occupancy in our Graybar Hotel. Arrestees are often amazed at the velocity at which the human body can be propelled (against its will) down a narrow hallway and into a small, dark, grungy cell.

10-8

I bagged a DUI on the highway the other day at 5:30 in the afternoon. It started as a loud muffler. Got upgraded to suspended vehicle registration. Moved on to a suspended driver's license. Threw in an open transport alcohol/driver. Graduated to a few failed sobriety tests and *Voila!* Driving under the influence/alcohol charge and a .16 Breathalyzer. When the dominoes fall, they fall.

10-8

How's this for a vicious cycle? Lawyers have to get their guilty criminal clients out of jail so the perps can commit more crimes so they can pay their lawyers.

10-8

Recently I arrested this guy who was passed out at the wheel while his car was parked on the shoulder of the highway. Our DUI laws allow us to arrest anyone who's in control of a motor vehicle on the highways of our state. They don't have to be driving. My arrestee wasn't too happy and pitched a bitch about it. He said, "Which would you rather have me be doing, driving in the condition I'm in right now or pulled off to the side of the road sleeping?" I said that obviously I thought the second option was safer. But hey, fella, you had to drive in that condition to get where you were before you pulled over. Not to mention what damage you might do if you woke up too early, started to drive, and then had a wreck. And by the way, being in control of a motor vehicle to me means sitting in the driver's seat of a driveable motor vehicle with the key in the ignition or in the hands of the motorist. To me, the car does not have to be running in these situations to constitute control. A lot of cops are very content to let motorists sleep it off there beside the road. Not me. In my mind, a sleeping drunk motorist poses a definite hazard. Because they did drive while drunk, they're an obstruction on the highway, and they could easily start up and become a real problem again. And I'm not going to wait, okay?

10-8

Many people from Southern California or Florida have no clue about how to drive in snowy, wintery weather conditions. And yet they attempt it anyway. Sliding around, fishtailing, no matter what happens they just keep driving. You'd think after about the second spin they'd pull over and rethink that winter driving thing. But nooooo.

10-8

The other night I got sent to this older couple's house in town, reference a motorist-assist. So I get there, and the husband and wife team are standing in their driveway scratching their heads. Here's their car, a $70,000 dollar European auto, stuck at the end of their drive in what appears to be one-quarter-inch of snow. No bull. Seventy thousand dollar car, stuck in one-quarter-inch of wet snow. So I do the public relations thing, dig a little with the shovel and then try to drive the car out. But I can't get the wheels to spin. Because I'm getting nowhere, I let the old lady drive while me and Hubby push. Only I'm just about having a coronary trying to push this baby because the wheels still won't spin. I'm pushing on a car that's stuck and won't move. So I'm yelling at the lady to step on the gas, and she's yelling back that she's got it floored and nothing is happening. So I got back in the car, and that's when I found out that the car has this new razzle-dazzle transmission computer-program thing. Essentially this stupid program says, "You get stuck in some wet snow or on some icy snow, tough shit, because I ain't gonna spin these wheels for you, baby!" Well, we finally managed to push that sucker out when the neighbors across the street came home and were kind enough to come over and give us the extra oomph we needed. Progress. I love it.

10-8

The poor coppers in the town north of us got stuck directing traffic at a major intersection on the highway when the traffic lights went out in the middle of a major snow storm. They used flares to illuminate the intersection, and thus accidentally set fire to the rubber portion of the median impact bumper guards. Oh, well.

10-8

Not long ago we had yet another chase in our town that ended up with the offender dying in a terrible wreck. This stuff appears to be on the rise. What a way to die, running from the police.

10-8

The other night, I arrested a twenty-year-old kid for traffic. While I was processing him, he told me a little about himself. He'd just gotten out of jail for a shooting incident for which he had to do about nine months. He told me that in high school he was offered both an athletic and an academic scholarship, but he just blew it. And judging by the circumstances surrounding my arrest of this individual, he's still blowing it. Don't blow it, kids. When opportunity knocks, latch onto it.

10-8

I backed up this rookie on a traffic arrest on the highway the other night. I volunteered to move the suspect vehicle off the road. That was a mistake. The rookie left with his arrestee, and it took me over fifteen minutes to get out of that car because the door locks were stuck. Did I feel stupid, or what? At least nobody saw me in my struggles, except a few very puzzled deer. At least I got out without breaking anything.

10-8

The *National Enquirer* had a brief article about some twenty-two-year-old kid who had accumulated more than $84,000 dollars in unpaid traffic citations and was suspended for fifty-six years. Now that's rough.

10-8

Every year we have a police officers' ball honoring our retired officers. I go because it's good to hear how they're doing and to know that there is life after cop-dom.

10-8

I heard a really shocking statistic on the radio just the other day. In some inner-city hospitals, almost 40% of all surgical patients are being treated for gunshot wounds.

10-8

I can still remember the last name of the cop who wrote me a speeding ticket fourteen years ago. I wonder if there are several, maybe hundreds, of people out there who remember me in such a fond manner.

10-8

One year I single-handedly defeated the high school senior class prank. I just happened to be cruising by the school at about 5:00 in the morning, right before graduation. I couldn't help but observe about 10,000 pounds of purloined crap from all over town stacked up on the front steps, with some egging and some nasty posters thrown in for good measure. I figured I could either report the mountain of crap, write up a lot of paper on the thing, and look like a jerk because it was my beat, or I could be inventive and take care of the problem some other way. I spent the next hour removing all traces of the kids' little project. No case, no embarrassment, no paper.

10-8

Just recently I set an all-time personal best on the cop job. I nabbed five bandits in five separate incidents in less than an hour. Oh, you might want to know that they were raccoons. And that I just happened to get stuck with animal-warden duty that day. But hey, a record is a record.

10-8

Yet another weird coincidence. This month I arrested a person from a certain address in our town. The very next night I arrested someone else from the address right next door! And it was by no means a high-crime neighborhood.

10-8

Most cops have at least one weakness. Me, I have a few. One of them is that I gotta have my Hostess cupcakes. I absolutely cannot go an entire eight-hour shift without gulping some cupcakes or Suzy-Qs or Twinkies. I've tried to cut down, but I just can't do it. I'm not overweight by any means, but there are probably other foods that are healthier for me, like brown rice and stuff. Right!

10-8

Cops and alcohol. I've spoken about this before, but I feel compelled to say more. We have a few coppers on our department who are embroiled in that battle with the bottle. It is a very sorry thing to see these guys come in to work looking like a truck ran over them and smelling like a gin mill. Okay, they do not usually show up to work drunk. But I just hate to see their general mental and physical health go down the tubes because they either can't see what they are doing to themselves or they can't or won't do anything about it. Each time I see them, I vow that I will never let that happen to me, regardless of what happens in my personal or professional life. This problem doesn't limit itself to the older guys. We've got a few younger guys headed down the same road, and they've only got a few years on.

10-8

There are two big ways to help a cop. On is to report crimes-in-progress and provide good descriptions. The other is when you are presented with the opportunity, the motive, and the know-how to commit a crime, don't do it!

10-8

One of our coppers rolled to assist on a man-with-a-gun call in a near-by town that just happened to be low on manpower at the time the call came out. When he arrived on the scene, he saw this drunk guy pointing a pistol and pulling the trigger, over and over. Nothing was happening, so he and another cop jumped the guy and disarmed him. It turned out that the gun was loaded, but the firing pin wasn't striking hard enought to fire the bullets. It was so close (a matter of less than a millimeter) that someone could easily have been shot or killed. It was just one of those lucky things.

10-8

Awhile ago one of our coppers had to shoot and kill a large vicious dog the attacked him on a call. The PD, in its infinite wisdom, decided to suspend this guy because he "should have carried his nightstick" on the call and just tried beating the dog to death while it ripped him apart instead of shooting. Great, just great.

10-8

I arrested this guy once for suspended driver's license who had what appeared to be (and from other evidence was) fresh needle marks on him. I talked to this guy for an hour or two. I was very saddened by seeing firsthand a human being of good character and potential caught up in this kind of situation. I treated him with dignity and respect. No lectures. When he was released, I wished him the best.

10-8

Not long ago this gal cop from a town nearby "slid" into an unusual situation. This poor jamoke she had to arrest on a traffic thing was being very cooperative. He told her straight out, "Uh, I've got a python under my jacket." Now I would be thinking, and I'm sure she was thinking, it's a revolver right, he's talking about a model of Colt gun. Wrong. It was winter, and the "arrestee to be" had a real python (as in big, very big snake) under his jacket, wrapped around his waist to keep it warm. Needless to say, said arrestee and coiled companion were transported together to the PD, where Mr. Python was warily placed in a bucket so he could be warm, happy, and by himself while "Jungle Jim" was booked.

10-8

The last day. I think about it sometimes. The last time I take the uniform off. It will be a major transformation for me, from guardian to ordinary citizen. I don't have any idea how I will take it. The "mantle of responsibility" will be removed from my shoulders the instant the gun comes off. In many ways, I will miss all the things that come with it. In many ways, I will not. But I will be secure in the knowledge that the vacuum I leave behind will not go unfilled. For there will be younger, stronger, smarter, more eager cops, better-trained and better-equipped, ready to pick up where I leave off. Ready to pick up that "mantle" I will relinquish. Ready to carry on. Despite all the beefing I do about this job, I believe it is an important one. It is an honor and a trust bestowed upon us by the people who live in our cities and towns. Every honest citizen who depends on us to defend the peace and uphold law and order can sleep tonight, secure in the knowledge that the guardianship will continue, unbroken. For we will always be there. Remember that, okay?

10-24

["Assignment Completed"]

About the Author

Officer X, a graduate of Purdue University, has served for twelve years as a police officer in a suburban department north of Chicago. He has received several commendations and is extremely active in drunk-driver enforcement. He is a long-time member of the Fraternal Order of Police and the Illinois Police Association. He is also a member of TOPS (the Top One Percent Society, an organization of people who score high on IQ tests). Divorced, he has two children from his second marriage. This is his first book.

Also Published by Calibre Press

BOOKS

TACTICS FOR CRIMINAL PATROL: [Available early 1995]
Vehicle Stops, Drug Detection & Officer Survival
by Charles Remsberg

How to turn ordinary traffic stops into felony arrests—and stay alive in the process. Includes little-known, insider strategies for identifying subtle criminal indicators, detecting deception, getting consent for searches, finding contraband, using K-9, expanding arrests, defeating deadly threats. **Law Enforcement Only.**

STREET SURVIVAL: $29.95
Tactics for Armed Encounters
by S. A. Ronald Adams, Lt. Thomas McTernan, Charles Remsberg

A wealth of practical information on how to avoid a shooting confrontation...and how to survive if one is unavoidable. Cited often in lawsuits as "the standard of performance" required of police officers today. **Law Enforcement Only.**

THE TACTICAL EDGE: $37.95
Surviving High-Risk Patrol
by Charles Remsberg

Advanced text with the most extensive collection of realistic tactical options for defeating violent offenders ever published. Used as foundation for much academy and in-service training and for promotional exams. **Law Enforcement Only.**

THE SATAN HUNTER $12.95
by Thomas W. Wedge

An expert's guide to Satanic and occult crimes. Includes how to detect evidence of Satanic worship, investigate crime scenes, interpret revealing signs and symbols, distinguish between real Satanic evidence and wanna-be vandalism. Useful for police, schools, concerned groups.

ROADSIDE SOBRIETY TESTS: $9.95
Making DUI Arrests Stand up in Court
by James Whitmore

Hip-pocket reference guide that helps put teeth into drunk-driving arrests. Details proven tactics for identifying DUIs, safely controlling vehicles and suspects, administering a multitude of court-defensible roadside tests, and testifying in court.

VIDEOS

SURVIVING EDGED WEAPONS $49.95
directed by Dennis Anderson

Life-saving tactics for controlling offenders who are armed with cutting and stabbing weapons. Covers everything from a suspect's pre-attack body language through what really works for defense. The most popular officer-survival training video ever.

ULTIMATE SURVIVORS: $49.95
Winning Against Incredible Odds
directed by Dennis Anderson

Gripping blockbuster on emotional survival after a crisis. Explores the remarkable lessons learned by 4 officers pushed to the absolute brink by violent encounters. Teaches the personal qualities needed to face devastating traumas with confidence and control. 12 film awards. Excellent to share with family members and civilian friends.

Order Today from Your Police Equipment Dealer or

CALIBRE PRESS, INC.
666 Dundee Rd., Suite 1607
Northbrook, IL 60062-2760

800-323-0037

(708) 498-5680 • FAX: (708) 498-6869

(Add $5 shipping/handling for first item, 50¢ for each additional item.
Double shipping for Canada, triple for overseas. Illinois residents add 8% tax.)

Also ask about our unique training programs and expert witness
services for law enforcement and corrections personnel.